The Seeker's Guide to
The Hidden Path

About the Authors

Raven Grimassi is an award-winning author of ten books on Wicca and Witchcraft, and has been a practitioner and teacher in these fields for over thirty-five years. Trained in both northern and southern European traditions, Raven brings a broad vision to the myths, legends, and symbolism of the Craft. Many of his writings have been seminal and foundational in the construction of various Craft traditions nationwide. Among his books are: *Beltane, Encyclopedia of Wicca & Witchcraft, Hereditary Witchcraft, Spirit of the Witch, Italian Witchcraft, Wiccan Magick, Wiccan Mysteries, The Witches' Craft, Witchcraft: A Mystery Tradition,* and *The Witch's Familiar.*

Stephanie Taylor has been a Witch at heart all of her life, and a tarot reader and spiritual counselor for over fifteen years. Currently she is co-director and teacher at the College of the Crossroads, a Mystery School dedicated to preserving and passing on the Old Ways. The College was founded in 2003 with author Raven Grimassi. Stephanie also operates Raven's Loft webstore and the Witch's Cottage shop at the College of the Crossroads.

About the Artist

Mickie Mueller is an artist, a practitioner of earth religion spirituality, and, since 2001, a Reiki healing master/teacher in the Usui Shiki Royoho tradition. Mickie's artwork has appeared in a variety of publications including cover art for *Witchcraft and Wicca* magazine in the United Kingdom, *Oracle 2000, Spirit Seeker,* and *Raven's Call* magazines.

The Seeker's Guide to
The Hidden Path

Raven
Grimassi
&
Stephanie
Taylor

Art by Mickie Mueller

Llewellyn Publications
Woodbury, Minnesota

First Edition
First Printing, 2007

Based on book design by Connie Hill
Cover art © 2007 and card images by Mickie Mueller
Cover design by Lisa Novak
Editing by Connie Hill
Llewellyn is a registered trademark of Llewellyn Worldwide, Ltd.

This book is a component of the The Hidden Path divination kit, which consists of a boxed set of 40 full-color cards, An organdy bag, and this perfect-bound book.
ISBN: 978-0-7387-1070-9

Llewellyn Publications
A Division of Llewellyn Worldwide, Ltd.
2143 Wooddale Drive, Dept. 978-0-7387-1070-9
Woodbury, Minnesota 55125-2989
www.llewellyn.com

Printed in the United States of America

In memory of our friend Maggie Macary

Other Books by Raven Grimassi and Stephanie Taylor

The Traveler's Guide to the Well Worn Path

CONTENTS

Contents

Introduction

With the countless divination decks available today, you may question why another one? In part the answer is that *The Hidden Path* is more than just a system of divination. One of the primary goals of this deck is to preserve, in simple imagery, the complex and inner teachings of Paganism, Wicca, and Witchcraft. In doing so, our goal was to join ancestral knowledge and wisdom with contemporary vision.

This quest first began with the development of *The Well Worn Path* divination deck. The challenge was then, as it remained for *The Hidden Path* deck, to create a universal appeal. This was challenging because different traditions use distinctive names for deities and festivals, which is also true for jointly shared concepts and tenets of belief. Another challenge was to decide what general theme connected to deities and their associated myths could be used without causing any particular tradition to feel excluded.

In the end we decided to take the key and central themes of pre-Christian European Paganism and match them (where possible) with contemporary reconstructions and eclectic gatherings as we commonly find them in modern practice. We felt that this approach honored both the past and present. However, we felt it important to present a cohesive system that made sense and provided a good foundation for people to establish their own practices. Our final decision was to provide a teaching system, which we title Ash, Birch, and Willow.

The system of Ash, Birch, and Willow is designed without specific emphasis on any individual tradition within any specific region of Europe. Instead, the system is designed to incorporate the commonality of the beliefs and practices shared by the majority of systems and traditions practicing today. One example is that no deity names appear on any of the card images. In place of names we are using titles such as the Lady of the Fields and the Lord of the Harvest. There are eight different titles assigned to each of the eight seasonal festivals, or Sabbats. The symbolism within each seasonal card is universal and can easily be embraced by any tradition.

The Hidden Path deck contains a mythos connected to the Otherworld, with an underlying current that follows a mated pair of goddess and god who journey together through the Wheel of the Year. The emphasis of this deck is upon the mystical and spiritual dimensions associated with Paganism, Wicca, and Witchcraft. In this light we are presenting the forty mystical concepts that vitalize modern traditions. *The Hidden Path* complements *The Well Worn Path*, which presented the forty foundational religious concepts. Together the two decks provide an entire and complete tradition for the solitary practitioner. In this sense, *The Hidden Path* can be viewed as an expansion deck (although it is a complete system that is not dependant upon *The Well Worn Path* deck). If you are interested in a deeper exploration of the Ash, Birch, and Willow system, we suggest reading *Witchcraft: A Mystery Tradition,* by Raven Grimassi.

When working with *The Hidden Path* deck you can experience the cards on different levels. This is because a great deal of magic and astral work went into the development of this deck. On a mundane level we drew upon ancient and modern sources to compile the written material. On an astral level we tapped into thought-forms that exist outside the material dimension. On a magical level we joined forces with our incredible artist, who mixed herbal tinctures into the materials used to create the images for this deck. The joining together of the three of us became something greater than the sum of its parts, and in the final analysis we believe that this deck was created through us and not by us.

About This Deck

Several years ago the idea for this deck was part of the system now known as *The Well Worn Path* divination deck. Because the concept was so unique at the time, the publisher wanted to introduce it in a forty-card format as opposed to the original proposal of eighty cards. To accomplish this we selected forty cards that depicted the foundational concepts of Paganism, Wicca, and Witchcraft.

The Well Worn Path deck was so well received that a decision was made to introduce an additional forty cards as *The Hidden Path* divination system. Like its predecessor, *The Hidden Path* is not a Tarot deck, but is instead a unique divination system designed specifically for the needs of modern Pagans, Witches, and Wiccans. It provides a system that presents themes that depict the spiritual Pagan culture of our European ancestors, and conveys the inner mysteries, concepts, and beliefs that are the roots of modern practice in Paganism, Wicca, and Witchcraft.

The Hidden Path deck is designed to serve as a solitary system as well as one that can be blended with *The Well Worn Path* divination deck. As noted earlier, *The Well Worn Path* presented the forty foundational aspects of Paganism,

Wicca, and Witchcraft. *The Hidden Path* presents the forty mystical aspects, and is, in effect, an expansion deck (both physically and spiritually). The cards can literally be shuffled into *The Well Worn Path* cards to create an eighty-card deck. However, *The Hidden Path* deck is also an independent tool and can be used without *The Well Worn Path*.

The title "The Hidden Path" was chosen to reflect the idea of secret wisdom preserved by our ancestors and passed to us as a spiritual lineage, as well as the connection to our world and beyond. The image is one of a path hidden in the woods that is guarded by the ash, oak, and thorn. Here our ancestors left us a magical gateway that opens to the sacred well containing the depth of their timeless secrets. The key is to remember that no mystery remains hidden to an open mind.

In *The Hidden Path* deck we have preserved and presented the important, vital, and viable traditions and beliefs that we all continue to honor into modern days. Here we have captured the knowledge and wisdom of ancient times for contemporary application. The design of each card has been carefully thought out and includes important and valuable symbolic imagery. The descriptions provide the reader with the tools and keys to access the hidden mysteries. The mystical teachings revealed in the cards are the connective links that together lead the reader to the entrance that opens to *The Hidden Path*. Now you will be able to use these relatable images for divination, ritual, personal alignment, path working, and teaching. It is our hope that your journey inward will lead you to the source of divine inspiration.

The Theme of This Deck

The theme that runs through this deck is associated with the myths and legends of the Otherworld. The images in *The Hidden Path* deck contain the essence of mystical concepts that are both ancient and modern. In this way the deck connects you with a living tradition that spans past, present, and future.

The essential theme begins with the idea of the Silver Bough and the Golden Bough. These sacred branches appear in ancient myth and legend where they grant safe passage to and from the Otherworld or Underworld. Those who carried the sacred bough entered the realm beyond in order to retrieve information, oracle power, or a magical vessel.

The mystical journey within the deck begins with the opening of the secret door, which is hidden from normal view. The setting for the majority of the cards in this deck takes place in the Otherworld where we find the Faery or Elven race. Here the reader is guided through an initiation experience that includes experiencing the eight festivals, or Sabbats, of the Wheel of the Year. In effect, the experience of this deck is within the Otherworld, which connects you directly with the astral impressions that empower each of the seasonal rites.

The eight festival cards depicted in this deck present a mated goddess and god pair. Together they journey through the Wheel of the Year in a shared mythical tale that brings a cohesive understanding to the divine presence within the seasons of Nature. Here the goddess and god have titles instead of names, which allow the user of the deck to relate to the images regardless of personal cultural preference. The storyline provided in the companion book to *The Hidden Path* deck, encourages the reader to experience herself or himself as the hero on a sacred quest in the Otherworld.

In the traditional tales of the hero who journeys to the Otherworld or Underworld, the figure must return to the world of mortal kind. It is the return of the hero that renews and revitalizes the people who await the reunion. In *The Hidden Path* deck, this important element is included in the theme of the cards. The last portion of the deck presents the portal of return from the Otherworld through the image of a cave tunnel leading back to the material world.

As you work with this deck you will find that the cards serve as alignments to Otherworld beings (the Elven or Faery), as well as bridges to the inner realms themselves. "Journey Through the Hidden Path" in this book (163–180) contains a guided image journey through each of the cards. This will aid in connecting you to the mystical themes reflected in the images.

In *The Well Worn Path* deck we presented the mystical figure known as the Crone of the Cottage. The images in that deck depicted her cottage, the surrounding grounds, and the mystical areas associated with ritual and magic. The journey included in that deck's companion book guided the reader through an encounter with the Crone of the Cottage, and then led the reader through the teachings associated with her realm.

The Hidden Path presents the gateway from the Crone's cottage into the Otherworld. In the Otherworld realm the reader is linked to transformational energies, which offer elevation and enlightenment. It is here that the collective consciousness and collective unconscious is preserved, blending the knowledge and experience of our ancestors with the evolved insights of their descendants. When you work with *The Hidden Path* deck, you are embracing the spiritual heritage passed to you from all the kindred souls who have trod the sacred path.

The theme of *The Hidden Path* deck brings the reader back into the Crone's cottage to experience the final connections that join his or her personal path to the work ahead that unites the tribe or community. It was mythologist Joseph Campbell who once pointed out that the inward journey leads us not to being alone, but instead opens for us the entire world.

How to Use This Deck

This deck is designed to serve several different purposes. It is a deck of divination, a system for teaching mystical concepts, and a tool for establishing spiritual alignments. The best way to learn about what this deck offers you is to first read the teachings and meanings associated with each card. This will familiarize you with the overall concept of each card, which is reflected in the symbolic representation.

Begin by looking at each card in this book and read only the section titled "Teaching." Next look at each card closely, study the imagery on it, and then turn to the next card. Continue in this manner until you have studied the teachings for each of the forty cards. In doing so you will see the emergence of a mystical theme that permeates the entire deck.

The next step is to return to the first card, and read the section titled "Divination Meaning." Continue reading through the forty cards as you did when reading the teaching sections. This exercise will fully integrate the symbolism and meaning of each card into your conscious and subconscious mind. Through this the need to memorize each card is minimized. Once you have completed the entire exercise you will find that the cards "speak" to you in a reading, and allow you additional insights into interpreting the reading.

The final step is to read the section for each card titled "The Shadow's Edge." There you will find the mystical teachings and associations represented in the card's imagery. These are the seeds of enlightenment that, once planted, will spring forth and bear fruit in the days ahead. Once you have read all the inner teachings, and studied the imagery on each card, a process is underway that will lead you to expanded vision and understanding. It is the full integration of the cards' imagery and theme, along with their entire cumulative effect, that will direct you along the path of enlightenment. That's the key to the inner teachings and mechanism of this deck as a spiritual tool.

Set up each card so you can easily view it, and then use it as a meditation based upon the theme presented in the text. Look at each card closely and read its message. Allow your mind to follow the threads. In this way the deck will provide you with a course of forty meditations in the mystical tradition.

When reading with these cards do not be limited to the scripted meaning for each one. Instead allow the imagery of each card—as well as the stated meaning—to contribute to the interpretation. As the cards are dealt out in a reading, each one will appear in different positions in the divination spread you select. The spreads (or layout designs) for this deck are the Looking Glass Spread, the Wheel of the Year, and the Three Realms Spread. Each position in a spread means something specific, and the card is interpreted by considering the meaning/imagery of the card as well as the meaning of the position it occupies.

Uses of the Deck

Divination Meaning

This section provides the basic meaning of each card for use in divination spreads. When a card appears in any position within a reading, look at it for a moment and allow the imagery to speak to you. Think about what you are seeing in the picture in terms of the expressed theme. Join the feeling you have about the imagery with the scripted meaning in this companion book. This combination becomes your understanding of the card in any reading. Lastly, interpret the stated meaning of the card in context with the meaning of the position on the layout spread where the card has turned up. Together, this will provide the message of the card in any given reading according to the layout.

Teaching

This section reveals the mystical, spiritual, or inner teachings of the concept represented in each card. Here the keys to understanding each aspect and tenet of belief within the Hidden Path system are preserved. You can deepen your understanding of the inner teachings by studying the connective cards. These are listed with each card, and by reading their teachings in connection with each other, the fragments become whole images of enlightenment.

Teachers and solitary students can use the cards in a type of "flash card" review to test comprehension and retention. Together, all of the cards in *The Hidden Path* present the forty mystical concepts that every Pagan, Witch, or Wiccan needs to know!

The Shadow's Edge

In this section are the enhancements that are related to the teachings provided in the "Teaching" section. Select one card and prop it up where you can be comfortable while viewing it. Read the "Teaching" section for the card and then read the "Shadow's Edge" text. Focus your attention on the card and allow your mind to drift through the symbolism. Try to stay within the mystical theme of the card. You can do this with two cards per week, and in this way you can engage in a spiritual and magical journey that will carry you through the year. For a deeper level of study, refer to the suggested cards that follow the Shadow's Edge section. These cards contain other layers of related teachings, which will help you integrate all the teachings together.

Journey Alignment

Included in this companion book is a section titled "Journey through the Hidden Path." Here you will find a story designed to provide you with an experience of each individual card. By reading through the story as directed, you will be spiritually aligned to the theme of each card. This alignment section will help you to gain a greater depth of awareness through guided imagery. Each card contains part of an ongoing story that will take you through a mystical journey using the deck of forty cards. The benefit of taking the journey is to help gain a deeper understanding of the significance of these important and vital traditional teachings. The goal of the journey is to align you with a chain of memory ideas that together form the pattern of the inner mysteries. It is through reflecting back upon the story, and the themes within the symbolism of the cards, that the mysteries are revealed.

Combine with *The Well Worn Path* Divination Deck

If you own a set of *The Well Worn Path* cards you will notice that *The Hidden Path* cards are the same size and share the same design on the back of the card. The images are also painted by the same artist, which allows for continuity of appearance. Because of these factors the cards can be shuffled together and used as a single deck.

The most unique aspect of *The Hidden Path* is that it can be combined with *The Well Worn Path* deck in several important ways. First, it will expand the deck to eighty cards to enhance the scope of divinatory possibilities. Second, it joins with the foundational concepts of *The Well Worn Path* deck with the mystical teachings of *The Hidden Path* deck. This provides the user with an entire system of teachings that comprise a complete and functional tradition of Paganism, Wicca, or Witchcraft.

A third aspect that arises when combining the two decks is the expansion of ritual application. In the companion book for *The Well Worn Path* you will find a complete ritual designed for either solitary full moon or Sabbat rituals/seasonal festivals. *The Hidden Path* deck provides eight beautiful seasonal depictions of the Sabbat rituals/seasonal festivials, which can be placed as the focal card in ritual structure of *The Well Worn Path*.

Customize the Deck

One of the many unique features of this deck is that you can customize the meaning of these cards to better reflect your own individual symbolism. Since these cards are not of Tarot design you can easily choose any meaning for them that appeals to you. The images in this deck are rooted in very old symbols and concepts. They represent ancestral imagery related to archetypal patterns. How you relate to these images may be different than the meanings we have provided in this book.

Once you have looked at the images on each of the cards, then you can decide whether the assigned meaning fits your personal feeling for each card image. If not, you can use your own feelings and personal symbolism to define what the images mean to you. This will help create a powerful and personal system of your own.

If you decide that you want to change the meaning of the card, it is relatively easy to do so. You can use a small sketchbook or notebook to write down your individual meaning for each card. This can serve as a type of Book of Shadows for your new deck. At the top of the page, write the name of the card. Below this write your meaning and any notes that you wish to include. Look through the cards, and note any new meanings. Perform several practice readings with the cards until it is easy to recognize what each card means to you. You can also keep a journal of the readings you do for yourself or others, and note any patterns that form or themes that run through them.

Divination Spreads

The deck features three divination spreads. Two of these reflect a mystical Pagan theme: the Three Realms Spread and the Wheel of the Year Spread. The third spread is designed to explore your everyday life and to look at future influences that can reshape it.

Using a spread design helps you focus the reading and conditions your psyche to interpret the cards as they appear in specific positions within the spread pattern. Each position in a spread has its own meaning. This will modify or enhance the meaning of the card that is placed in each position. It is therefore important to interpret each card in conjunction with the context of what the position represents.

Looking Glass Spread

This card spread is designed for an overview of the important areas in the life of the average person. These areas include career, money, love, fortune, and various relationships. The spread uses twenty-one cards, dealt into seven groups of three cards. Each grouping reveals information that pertains to the theme of each area of life.

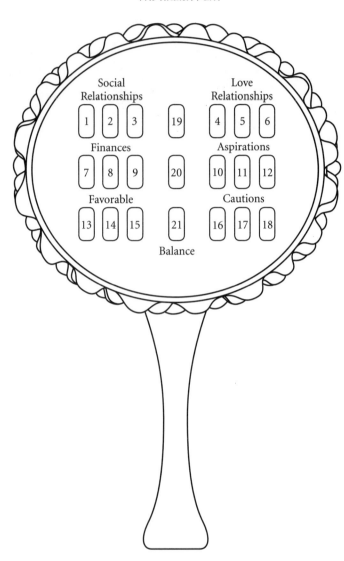

Looking Glass Spread

Begin the reading by shuffling the cards seven times. Then, using the illustration, deal out the cards face down in the numbered sequence. Next, turn up cards in the one, two, and three position. Look at the meanings of each card. Their placements are in the zone of social relationships, and are interpreted in the following context:

Social Relationships

One: people influencing your life
Two: actions, intentions, or motives of these people
Three: whether they are allies or enemies

Repeat this formula for each zone as follows:

Love Relationships

Four: your true feelings toward the desired person
Five: what is at the core of the desire
Six: how the other person feels about you

Finances

Seven: gain or loss
Eight: what is important to assure finances
Nine: what can aid or obstruct

Aspirations

Ten: state of mind
Eleven: status of plans and goals
Twelve: focal point

Favorable Influences

Thirteen: what can be gained or overcome
Fourteen: allies or connections that assist
Fifteen: areas that need improvement to gain success

Cautions

Sixteen: who or what to guard against
Seventeen: areas to avoid or approach with special care
Eighteen: what can help offset problems ahead

Balance

The cards in this section are positioned between two areas of life. For example, number nineteen is between social relationships and love relationships. Think of these cards as bridges that connect the two areas, but more importantly, think of them as what can bring needed balance to these areas (whether to enhance the positive or offset the negative).

Nineteen: what is needed to balance nonromantic relationships with romantic ones
Twenty: what is needed to balance finances with goals
Twenty-One: what is needed to balance favorable influences against negativity

These last three cards and their positions provide a comprehensive view of the entire reading.

Wheel of the Year Spread

This card spread is designed to take you on a journey through the twelve months of the Wheel of the Year. Each card will reflect the events and influences for each month. We recommend beginning the reading on an auspicious date such as your birthday, a new moon, or a full moon. Each month you will explore a card and how it reflects upon your life. The interpretation of the card can be divinatory or can be used spiritually for path working.

Begin by shuffling the cards, separating them into three stacks to the left, and then stack them one on top of the other. Do this in any order that feels right to you, but move the stacks to the left as you reassemble them. A total of twelve cards is used in this layout, each one representing an individual month in your coming year.

Deal the cards out, face down, in the circular pattern shown in the illustration spread. Begin by placing the first card at the left hand side position marked number one. Then, moving counterclockwise, place eleven cards to complete the circle. Once the circle is completed the meaning of the twelve cards will address the twelve months of your year.

This spread can also be used to coincide with the phases of the moon, and in this way you can watch for the lunar influences. For example, you may wish to begin the spread with the new moon of September. In this case, the first card will be read to indicate the time period from September's new moon to the new moon in October. During this time the meaning or teaching can serve as a focal point for

Wheel of the Year Spread

growth and transformation, typically about twenty-eight days. The second card is then dealt and applies from the October new moon through the November new moon and so on through a twelve-month period.

You may wish to use the date of a birthday or anniversary, and create a reading for the months ahead. If, for example, the date is April 18, then the first card spans the period from April 18 to May 18, and the next card would apply from May 18 to June 18, and so on. You may even wish to lay out a card spread beginning with one full moon in a specific month and then from full moon to full moon as they appear throughout the year.

One of the purposes of this spread is to use the cards as magical pathworking tools as well as doorways to divinatory exploration. Each month gives you an opportunity to observe, grow, develop, and fine-tune your life in respect to the card with which you are working. By laying out the cards in the Wheel pattern you can discern patterns unfolding, in respect to the year, at a glance. Many times the bottom six cards of the Wheel will reveal challenges to move through, while the top six cards will reveal opportunities for personal achievements. Use the teaching or divinatory description for each card as a guideline to transform your life by aligning yourself to the card during the month in which it appears in the reading.

To expand and enhance a reading that is already dealt out, select the card for the month about which you want more information. Place it off to the side and then shuffle the rest of the deck. Next, deal out five cards in the pattern of a pentagram around the selected card. These five cards will represent the five elemental influences of earth, air, fire, water, and spirit upon the focal card for the month. Examine the meaning of each card and apply it as an elemental influence. For example, let's consider the Oak King card in each of the elemental placements and how to best interpret it.

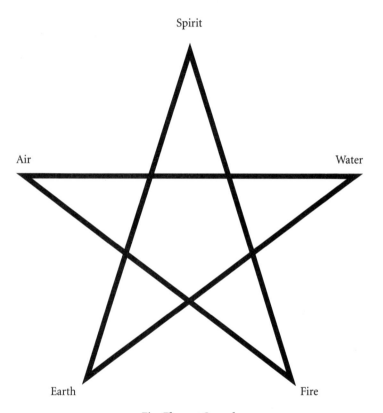

Five Element Spread

In the earth position, the Oak King indicates a foundational increase or a material gain. In the air position, it represents creative visions and insights. In the fire position, the Oak King symbolizes beneficial transformations and changes. In the water position, it speaks about movement in a gainful direction, or addresses positive emotions. The position of spirit symbolizes the driving or directing force, and here the Oak King indicates that a higher nature is emanating positive energy intended for growth.

Using the example of the Oak King, apply the elemental nature to any card's influence when it is dealt out in the pentagram pattern. Sometimes the meaning will be positive and sometimes challenges will appear. In any case, the pentagram pattern will give you greater insights into any of the cards in the Wheel of the Year Spread.

Three Realms Spread

This spread is designed to explore your current situation, the spiritual influences from above, and the challenges that are the roots of what you draw into your life experience. The concept behind this spread is connected to the teaching of the soul contract. This is a belief that the soul enters into each life with a specific plan, purpose, and goal. However, there are factors that aid as well as challenge the successful completion of the soul contract.

The Three Realms Spread can aid in viewing and discerning the progress of the soul contract by examining what is transpiring on different levels. On a mundane level the spread can also enhance your understanding of conditions

Three Realms Spread

related to relationships, career, finances and other areas of your life.

Look at the illustration and you will note three zones into which the cards are placed. The area of the branches and leaves represents the higher nature or the divine influences that help guide and direct. The area of the tree's trunk symbolizes the world in which you live, and the influences that are contributing to the condition of your life. The area of the roots applies to very deep patterns that arise not only from past-life experiences, but also from trauma in the current life. Often this trauma comes from early childhood, or from events associated with sexuality and well-being (physically, emotionally, and spiritually).

To use this spread, deal the cards out, face down, in the pattern detailed in the illustration. Within the tree trunk the positions indicate:

1. Physical

2. Mental

3. Spiritual

4. Emotional

Turn up the card in the number one position and refer to its divinatory meaning. Look at the imagery of the card and allow it to speak to you with the inner voice (what is the picture saying to you about a physical condition?). Once you have considered the scripted meaning, and then discerned the feeling you get from the picture on the card, render your interpretation of what the card is saying. In essence this number placement is about the general health and well-being of the individual. This can also apply to material success.

Repeat this interpretation formula for each of the remaining areas: mental, spiritual, and emotional. Once you have thought about the meaning of the four cards regarding each category, put the meanings together as you look for an overall view of the condition of the person in the reading.

The next step is to turn up the cards in the number positions five, six, seven, and eight. Within the branches the positions indicate:

5. What divine or higher forces affix to the soul in material life

6. The influence on the soul regarding its ability to communicate, convey, and create

7. How change is directed or maintained regarding the soul's experience in life

8. How compassion, love, and empathy surround the soul in life

Turn up the card in the number five position and refer to its divinatory meaning. Look at the imagery of the card and feel what it is conveying—what is the picture saying to you about what has been attached to the soul as a physical or material condition? This can include social status. Once you have considered the scripted meaning, and discerned the feeling generated from the picture on the card, render your interpretation of the card's meaning. In essence this number placement is about the life conditions that the soul has entered into, which can include financial status, handicaps, physical advantages, talents, and other things that can aid or challenge the experience of material life. Look for the relationship between card numbers one and five. This can help determine the outcome of what position one signifies when the higher nature is factored in, which means that the long-term effects of the five position will prevail.

Repeat this interpretation formula for positions six, seven, and eight. The card in the six position will show what influences emanate from above and how this aids or challenges the soul with communication skills and creativity related to the mind (arts, sciences, and so forth). The card in position seven will reveal how the soul is aided or challenged in terms of causing or experiencing changes in life. This can be both outer and inner, and can even indicate whether the soul can cause changes in communities and other people, perhaps even in the world. The card in position eight shows how is the soul is aided or challenged by its spiritual gifts or spiritual wounds. This is an important placement, as it is often a key to what the soul needs to accomplish in order to shed its karmic attachment.

The final phase of the Three Realms Spread is the area of the roots of the tree. This area is the subconscious, as well as the soul memory of past lives. It is here that you draw upon your strengths and what nourishes you. But here also you draw upon your fears and what has injured you. This is the place of deep shadows, and these shadows enfold the light of liberation.

Turn up the cards in the number nine, ten, eleven, and twelve positions. Within the roots these positions indicate:

9. What sets and sustains the material condition

10. What connects, draws in, and sends out

11. What brings the element of change and transformation

12. What causes flux and flow—or the lack thereof

Turn up the card in the number nine position and refer to its divinatory meaning. Look at the imagery of the card and feel what it is conveying: what is the picture saying to you about what keeps feeding your physical or material condition? Once you have considered the scripted meaning, and interpreted the feeling generated from the picture on the card, render your interpretation of the card's meaning. In essence, this number placement is about past conditions that have affected the soul—these can include financial status, physical conditions, and the enjoyment of life in family, career, and relationships. Look for the relationship between card numbers one, five, and nine, as these are all earth elemental influences. This can help you work toward a resolution or increased understanding of how divine emanations combine with bound energies from the past that are still carried.

Once the cards are dealt out and interpreted, you can repeat the comparisons of mated cards that share an elemental nature:

Earth: one, five, nine

Air: two, six, ten

Fire: three, seven, eleven

Water: four, eight, twelve

By studying these triple matings in each elemental influence, you can discern how your life is being influenced from above and below. This will allow you to take advantage of your strengths and gifts, while at the same time learning how to handle and adjust to the challenges that have attached themselves to your life in this present incarnation.

The Cards

Sacred Bough

DIVINATION MEANING

When this card appears, a course of action is indicated. An important decision is at hand, and it is one that can reshape the future. When the reading is about choices or chances, this card assures us that the tools and keys are within reach to accomplish what needs to be done.

Keywords

Quest, Journey, Chosen Path.

TEACHING

The Sacred Bough appears in old myths and legends in both northern and southern Europe. In the north is it often called the "Silver Bough." It is often described as bearing apples, and the faery queen presents the silver bough to mortals. This assures safe passage to and from the Otherworld. In southern Europe the branch is known as the "Golden Bough," taken from a sacred oak tree bearing mistletoe. A mystical woman known as a sybil gives the golden bough to mortals, and it ensures safe passage to and from the Underworld.

SACRED BOUGH

The card depicts a tree from whose branches are suspended the sacred silver and golden boughs. These are the choices or opportunities one can grasp. A key hangs upon a cord, representing that the way can be opened. The colored cord (red, black, white) symbolizes the three great mysteries of birth, life, and death. On the trunk near the branches is the Wheel of Hecate, which symbolizes the presence of divinity where your roads of opportunity divide into two separate paths. At the base of the tree are offerings, reminding us to be mindful that something must be given in order for something else to be received.

THE SHADOW'S EDGE

The Sacred Bough card speaks to us of the inner journey. The connection in the card's theme to female agents indicates the intuitive, psychic, and subconscious levels of communication. Through the imagery of the card we find that other dimensions exist outside of the constructed world in which we live our daily lives. We need only to risk the journey.

The Sacred Bough assures us that death is not required in order to experience the reality of existence outside of the flesh. It demonstrates that we can depart and return through the directed will of our minds and hearts, which are the branch and the roots of our own inner sacred bough.

For inner connection, see these cards: Oak, Ash and Thorn; Faery Door; Otherworld; Elder Staff.

Oak, Ash and Thorn

DIVINATION MEANING

When this card appears, it addresses a situation that is blocked or guarded. Special actions or attitudes are required in order to gain entrance or passage.

Keywords

Guarded, Secret, Hidden.

TEACHING

The oak, ash, and hawthorn trees are legendary guardians that bar the way into the Otherworld. The oak and ash stand as the portals at the threshold. The hawthorn, with its sharp spikes, guards against easy access. Between the ash and the oak is the in-between place, which is neither in this world nor in the next. It is a place of magic, where anything is possible.

The card depicts an ash tree (left) and an oak tree (right). In the center of the card is a hawthorn tree, which is blocking the opening between the ash and oak. The upper branches of the ash and oak form an archway, suggesting

OAK, ASH AND THORN

the presence of a portal to another realm beyond. From this vantage point spirits watch all who approach.

THE SHADOW'S EDGE

The Oak, Ash and Thorn card informs us that some things are kept from us until we prove ourselves worthy. Worthiness can take many forms, and the most important are ethics, maturity, integrity, compassion, and courage. In the mystery tradition, the seeker is often drawn into a situation wherein he or she is challenged. The way can be opened in such an encounter, or the seeker can become entangled in the process itself and become lost. This is reflected in folk tales where a person's curiosity results in their being "faery led" into a thicket. Clarity of vision, strength of purpose, and personal integrity are needed to pierce the mysteries.

For inner connection, see these cards: Faery Door; Between the Worlds; Otherworld; The Kindred; Sacred Bough.

Faery Door

DIVINATION MEANING

When this card appears, it is a sign that something is finally revealed or accessible now. Obstacles are removed and the way forward is clear for the traveler. However, the journey ahead holds unexpected gains and delights that will have a profound effect.

Keywords

Entry, Passage Way, Opportunity.

TEACHING

The faery door is a legendary point of passage between the world of mortal kind and the realm of the faery race. It is often depicted as hidden in tree trunks or earthen mounds. Sometimes a secret password is required to open a faery door, and in some stories the ringing of a bell or the playing of a musical instrument is needed.

The card depicts a magical doorway appearing between the ash and oak trees. In the foreground the hawthorn has parted its thorny branches, revealing what was previously hidden. The doorknob is shaped like an apple (the fruit of

FAERY DOOR

the faery world), and signifies that this entry point leads to another reality outside of the mundane world. Mounted on the door is the triple symbol, which represents the unity of the three points that mark the triangle of manifestation: time, space, and energy. When all three are present anything can be accomplished.

THE SHADOW'S EDGE

The Faery Door card is a sign that magical opportunities present themselves in our lives. These are junctures of Fate that can be pivotal moments. Through this we understand that divinity takes an active role in guiding our lives. We must realize that it opens doors and reveals vistas, but it doesn't force us to take the required actions. Everything we do, or fail to do, creates a ripple that alters our future.

This is why our goals and actions must be noble.

For inner connections see these cards: Sacred Bough; Oak, Ash and Thorn; The Kindred; Samhain; Chthonic Roots; Astral Body; Three Great Realms; Litha.

Between the Worlds

DIVINATION MEANING

When this card appears, it suggests that your vision is not yet clear enough to manifest your desire. There are too many ideas, distractions, or daydreams in sight. Manifestation requires clarity and a better focus. The card may also indicate a delay in plans unfolding. Things are in the works but more is needed to accomplish the goal.

Keywords

Visualization, Imagination, Transmission.

TEACHING

A dimension exists between the world of material matter and the realm of astral form. According to this belief, every material object was originally an astral form before it could become a physical object. The "World between the Worlds" is a corridor that connects both dimensions (material and astral). Energy flows to and from the inner astral dimension, and is sometimes depicted as a river. This symbolic river carries visualized desires from the material world into the astral realm. Here they take on a representa-

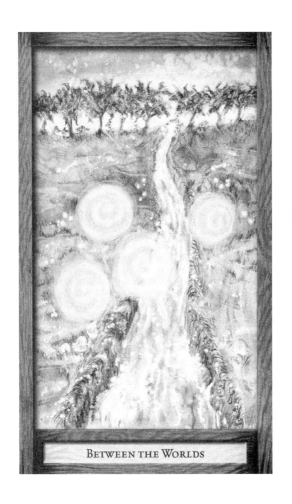

BETWEEN THE WORLDS

tive form and then flow back into the material realm where the "formed-thought" becomes the object or situation that it illustrates.

The card depicts a mystical realm with a river flowing into the horizon. This symbolizes the flow of energy from the material world into the astral realm. The river carries "thought-forms" created by ritual and magic, which are transported into the astral fabric where they can take shape. Once formed, these astral images are carried back into the material realm where they manifest the desires of their creators.

Hovering above the river are four spheres, which are sometimes called faery orbs or soul orbs. They represent the presence of beings that can travel back and forth between the worlds at will. In this sense they can aid the ritual or magical desires that flow between the worlds. This is one reason why offerings are often made to spirits when performing ritual or magic.

The realm depicted on this card appears as a crossing point between material and spirit. This is because this corridor separates each definable dimension, existing in-between. It is here that a desire moves toward manifestation or ebbs away and disappears. The latter is typical of daydreams, which have no drive of energy behind them.

THE SHADOW'S EDGE

The Between the Worlds card expands our consciousness to an awareness that material existence is only a part of reality. Peering between the worlds allows us to see the inner mechanism that operates within nature. Through this we can perceive the cycles, tides, and flows of energies that wash across the planes of existence. It is here, between the worlds, that we can meet with beings and realms that exist just outside the border of our limited awareness. Expansion of vision and the evaluation of self-imposed limitations are essential for spiritual growth.

For inner connections see these cards: Art of Magic; Otherworld; Samhain; Kindred; Astral Body; Watchers.

The Kindred

DIVINATION MEANING

When this card appears, it means that the needed connections are there, allies are awaiting your call, and you have the support needed. It is time to call for aid. The card can also mean that teachings are about to come from higher sources.

Keywords

Allies, Guides, Co-Workers.

TEACHING

Ancient myths and legends tell of the Faery or Elven race. In many tales they are allies of mystics, witches, shamans, and other seekers of the inner mysteries. Traditionally the doorways between the world of mortal kind and the faery realm open at the equinox and solstice periods.

These kindred beings are spiritual allies who willingly work with mortals in order to ensure the balance between the worlds. What happens to one dimensional realm affects all others, and the state of the material world can have significant impact on nonmaterial realms. This is why the

THE KINDRED

kindred first came to teach mortals the ancient arts, and to establish certain sects as the caretakers or custodians of the material world. Among these sects are the pagans, druids, witches, occultists, and shamans.

The card depicts four faery or elven beings. They appear in the light that emanates from their mystical realm. Each wears a circlet upon the forehead, denoting their office as teachers and guides to the inner mysteries.

THE SHADOW'S EDGE

The Kindred card reveals that we are not alone in the Universe. Beings exist beyond and outside of the material realm. Spiritual fellowships exist that serve beings in earlier stages of evolution through the planes of existence. The spiritual beings within such groups are sometimes called spirit guides, guardians, and allies. Communication and interaction with these beings is possible through dreams and meditations. Forming rapport and relationships with spiritual beings is an aid to our spiritual evolution.

For inner connections, see these cards: Otherworld; Faery Door; Sacred Site; Litha; Samhain; Oak, Ash and Thorn.

Otherworld

DIVINATION MEANING

When this card appears, it indicates that the time has come to move on. The current situation must be released, as it is no longer viable. Look to and move toward new horizons.

Keywords

Transition, Journey, Crossing.

TEACHING

In ancient myth and legend there is a realm known by such names as Avalon, Tir Nan Og, the Elysian Fields, or the Summerland. In pre-Christian European paganism such realms are referred to as the Otherworld (or Underworld). Here is the realm of the faery or elven race, a dimension existing outside of the material world. It is sometimes called the Eternal Land. The Otherworld is free of illness, disease, old age, and death.

The card depicts a faery woman sailing into a mystical fog, which parts as three swans are directed ahead. Through the opening can be seen the white shores of the Otherworld, and on the island a castle rises atop the rocky cliff.

OTHERWORLD

THE SHADOWS'S EDGE

The Otherworld card speaks to us of hidden realms beyond the material senses. It is through this understanding that we arrive at the realization that we are spiritual beings moving through experiences in many dimensions. Physical life is the seed that becomes the blossom that eventually dies to become new seed (and therefore new life). It is only when we part the veil that we can see existence beyond the material experience. This is the liberation of knowing that physical death is not the end.

For inner connections, see these cards: Oak, Ash and Thorn; Faery Door; The Kindred; Three Great Realms; Sacred Bough.

Oak King

DIVINATION MEANING

When this card appears, a person or situation arises or arrives that can lead you to success, gain, and growth.

Keywords

Gain, Growth, Increase.

TEACHING

In northern European lore we find the character known as the Oak King. He personifies the waxing period of the year, which runs from the winter solstice through to the summer solstice. In his legends, the Oak King fights his brother (the Holly King) for rule of the year. The Oak King wins the winter solstice battle, and the Holly King wins the summer solstice fight.

In southern European lore the equinox periods mark the waxing and waning periods of the year. The seasonal changes are personified by the stag (at the spring equinox) and the wolf (at the autumn equinox).

The card depicts the Oak King dressed in woodland clothing and wearing an oak wreath crown. He holds a staff

OAK KING

that bears a carved stag's head. On his chest he wears a medallion of amber and jet that signifies his time of power.

THE SHADOW'S EDGE

The Oak King addresses the theme of prosperity as a cycle of its own in nature. It assures us that even as decline and death is certain, so too is the certainty of renewal and new life. The Oak King personifies the divine consciousness within this cycle of nature, which is testimony to the tenacity of the principles represented in the waxing season of the year.

For inner connections, see these cards: Litha; Yule; Holly King; Tree in Spring; Tree in Summer.

Holly King

DIVINATION MEANING

When this card appears, it signals a person or situation arising or arriving that can bring about release, decline, dissolution, or loss.

Keywords

Decline, Loss, Dissipation.

TEACHING

In northern European lore we find the character known as the Holly King. He personifies the waning period of the year, which runs from the summer solstice through to the winter solstice. In his legends, the Holly King fights his brother (the Oak King) for rule of the year. The Holly King wins the summer solstice battle, and the Oak King wins the winter solstice fight.

In southern European lore the equinox periods mark the waxing and waning periods of the year. The seasonal changes are personified by the stag (at the spring equinox) and the wolf (at the autumn equinox).

HOLLY KING

The card depicts the Holly King dressed in winter clothing and wearing a holly wreath crown. He holds a staff that bears a carved wolf's head. On his chest he wears a medallion of amber and jet that signifies his time of power.

THE SHADOW'S EDGE

The Holly King presents the theme of decline as a cycle of its own in nature. It assures us that even as life and the return of life is certain, so too is the certainty of decline and death. The Holly King personifies the divine consciousness within this cycle of nature, which is testimony to the tenacity of the principles represented in the waning season of the year.

For inner connections, see these cards: Litha; Yule; Oak King; Tree in Fall; Tree in Winter.

Sacred Sight/Site

DIVINATION MEANING

When this card appears, it indicates a need to narrow your vision in order to discover what is at the core of what you seek. It can also mean that you will be guided toward what is needed in your journey or quest.

Keywords

Focus, Direction, Alignment.

TEACHING

The ancient Hag Stone is a mysterious figure often appearing as a large standing stone with a hole through it. When peering through the opening, we see that the Hag Stone is aligned to focus on a particular site that holds religious or magical significance. It is very common for a Hag Stone to direct the vision toward a "faery path," "ley line," or a classic crossroads.

The card depicts a standing Hag Stone with a ritual circle in sight through the hole. Behind the circle stands an old tree. This is a sacred place where magic and rituals have been performed beneath the full moon for countless centu-

SACRED SIGHT/SITE

ries. Upon close examination the moss pattern on the Hag Stone resembles an eye, a mystical symbol of vision.

THE SHADOW'S EDGE

The Sacred Sight/ Site card speaks to us of directed vision. This relates to both the internal and external. The material dimension exerts a great deal of energy upon the sensory elements of physical life. This can distract the soul from what it needs to seek out and experience while dwelling within a material body. In this regard the card reminds us that sign posts and directional aids are always there before us in the spiritual journey. We need only look with focused vision upon the goals we need to accept and achieve.

For inner connections, see these cards: Faery Door; The Kindred; Otherworld; Sacred Grotto.

Priestess and Priest

DIVINATION MEANING

When this card appears, it indicates a need for mentorship and guidance, and is a sign not to rely solely upon oneself.

Keywords

Mentorship, Alliance, Guidance.

TEACHING

The role of the priestess or priest is to serve as clergy and counsel for their community. Traditionally, the priestess and priest perform initiation rituals and direct the training of initiates within their system. These individuals pass on their teachings and experience to others.

The card depicts a faery or elven priestess and priest who appear from the Otherworld. The priestess holds a sacred chalice, the symbol of the female vessel of manifestation. The priest holds a wand, the symbol of directional manifestation. Together they stand and gesture a welcome to accompany them on the path.

PRIESTESS AND PRIEST

THE SHADOW'S EDGE

The Priestess and Priest card is another indication of spiritual beings in the category of guides and allies. The emphasis of this card is upon the religious and spiritual aspects of the Otherworld fellowship. It is through this imagery that we can connect with those who would guide us to alignments that empower our understanding of deity. Through a deepening of our understanding, we can better interact and interface with the divine source of creation. Merging with the source brings the soul into a comprehension of its purpose in the divine plan, which gives the soul direction along the path of spiritual evolution.

For inner connections, see these cards: Charge of the Goddess; Great Rite; Karma; Drawing Down the Moon.

Drawing Down the Moon

DIVINATION MEANING

When this card appears, it is a sign to be open and to "rise above" and seek a higher nature. Doing so may require becoming a vessel to draw and contain what is needed to accomplish what you seek. It can also indicate the awakening or strengthening of oracle or psychic abilities.

Keywords
Higher Vision, Expanded Perspective.

TEACHING

In modern times, drawing down the moon refers to invoking the Goddess within the mind and body of the High Priestess. This is performed in a ritual circle on the night of the full moon. The High Priestess then serves as the vessel for the Goddess through which she may speak and interact with her followers.

In the earliest mentions of drawing the moon down from the sky we find the concept of using the moon's light. Dew was collected from moss or lichen at dawn on the morning following the night of the full moon. Ancient Roman writers

DRAWING DOWN THE MOON

such as Lucan refer to this magical substance as the foam of the moon.

The card depicts a High Priest kneeling in front of a High Priestess. He invokes the Moon Goddess into her body. In the background the Goddess is seen manifesting during the invocation. The High Priest wears a crown with antler tips, which denote his connection with the woodland God of the forest. The High Priestess wears a circlet bearing the symbols of the full moon, waxing moon, and waning moon. The circlet is a sign of her rapport and connection to the feminine divine.

The triangle figure of the priest's hands represents the Triangle of Manifestation, which marks time, space, and energy. These are the three requirements for manifestation to take place. Traditionally, to assist the High Priestess with invoking the Goddess, the High Priest uses the ritual wand to trace a triangle on her body, using the nipples and genital area as the three corners of the triangle. This creates an inverted triangle into which the Goddess pours like water into a cup, taking on the shape of the container.

THE SHADOW'S EDGE

The Drawing Down the Moon card deals with the concept of the receptive vessel and the vehicle for channeling. This concept relates to the necessity of a material form through which a spirit being can operate within the material dimension. This is similar to possession, with the exception that possession can be involuntary or undesired, whereas the act of drawing down the moon is a willful and purposeful act of opening up to receive the emanation of divine consciousness.

For inner connections, see these cards: Otherworld; Sacred Site; Priestess and Priest; Astral Body; Art of Magic; Centers of Power; Elder Staff; Sacred Grotto; Charge of the Goddess.

Great Rite

DIVINATION MEANING

When this card appears, it indicates a consummation, a joining together beyond personal matters or limitations. It can also point to the perfect union formed to create something greater than the parts can be on their own.

Keywords

Perfect Union, Soul Mates, Divine Match.

TEACHING

The Great Rite represents the union of divine polarities, which are traditionally viewed as masculine and feminine. These are personified as God and Goddess. In some traditions a couple performs an initiation rite that includes sexual intercourse, which consummates a divine marriage of the masculine and feminine forces. This divine marriage is known as the Hieros Gamos. In other traditions the ritual is performed symbolically, using such tools as the chalice and wand, or chalice and blade. These represent the active (wand or blade) and receptive (chalice) forces. Traditionally, the chalice represents the feminine womb, and the

Great Rite

GREAT RITE

67

wand represents the phallus. In some modern traditions the blade (athame) has replaced the wand.

The card depicts a wand being dipped into a chalice. A man holds the wand of the masculine polarity and a woman holds the chalice of the feminine polarity. Both people wear a cord around their wrists, symbolizing the handfasting or wedding that unites the couple as one.

THE SHADOW'S EDGE

The Great Rite card takes up the idea of mimicry magic. This is the belief that by portraying something, a person can thereby attract what is represented. In the case of the Great Rite, the desire is to invoke the essence of the union of the divine polarities (Goddess and God). In other words, this is performed to establish an inner alignment wherein the masculine and feminine aspects of the divine source make a connection with the soul. Through this act the soul joins in a moment of oneness with the source from which it originated. Arising from this union, we can comprehend and experience the opposite gender polarity within, which helps us integrate our own feminine and masculine aspects.

For inner connections, see these cards: Drawing Down the Moon; Beltane; Litha; Mortar and Pestle; Priestess and Priest.

Tree in Winter

DIVINATION MEANING

When this card appears, it is a sign that preservation is needed. Conserve, stay put, and endure.

Keywords

Endurance, Preservation, Stability.

TEACHING

The Tree in Winter symbolizes endurance and preservation, and tells us to conserve when we find ourselves in the barren season of our life. A tree in winter does not hate the cold nor mourn the loss of its leaves. It stands as a tree in winter, embracing what is natural to the conditions surrounding it, while it awaits the ensured renewal of the coming spring.

The card depicts the dead of winter with a tree devoid of its leaves, its branches covered with snow. A wolf approaches, symbolizing the season of decline. To the right in the snow are the hoofprints of a stag, the symbol of the waxing season.

TREE IN WINTER

THE SHADOW'S EDGE

The Tree in Winter card speaks to us of preserving and preparation. As a mystery teaching this applies to the barren times of spirituality when a person feels cut off from divinity, community, or even oneself. The message of the tree in winter is to hold onto those things that remain, and to accept what is sparse without feelings of negativity or deprivation. When we focus on preparation then the message is that something else is on the horizon. Such thoughts and feelings draw us into the spiritual spring season.

For inner connections, see these cards: Imbolc; Holly King.

Yule/Winter Solstice

DIVINATION MEANING

When this card appears, it indicates a time of birth, which brings newness. New light is cast, new choices and chances can now appear. The card can also mean enlightenment coming from a new source.

Keywords

Rebirth, Renewal, Restoration.

TEACHING

Yule is the time of the rebirth of the Sun God, whose new light and life will revitalize the earth and all living things. He is born to the Great Goddess who gives birth to all things, and to whom all things return at the end of their time.

The card depicts the ritual setting of the Yule festival, which is marked by the winter solstice. Statues of the Goddess and God appear behind an altar, with the sun rising at dawn. The God is decorated with the red, black, and white woven cords of the mystery tradition. Red represents the living blood of our ancestors, which flows in our veins. Black represents the deep shadows that contain the enlight-

YULE/WINTER SOLSTICE

enment awaiting the true seeker. White symbolizes what remains behind, a metaphor of the bone, representing the wisdom and knowledge left behind by our ancestors.

Along with the cord are holly, pinecones, and mistletoe in honor of the solar season of his birth. In his hand the God holds a woven reed sun disk, a symbol of his divine solar nature. Sacred mistletoe hangs suspended from a cord around the waist of the God.

A lighted candle sits on the Goddess statue, representing her divine presence, and at her feet is the cauldron of rebirth from which the birthing fire of the sun rises.

Between the statues, the altar bears the sacred Yule log with three candles that represent the triformis aspects of the God (Hooded One, Horned One, and Old One). Around the log are pine boughs, pinecones, mistletoe, and holly representing the woodland nature of the God and his connection to the plant kingdom. In front of the altar is a reed basket containing a reed doll, symbolic of his ancient association with wetlands. The doll represents the figure known as the Child of Promise, who returns warmth and light to a world grown dark and cold with winter.

THE SHADOW'S EDGE

The Yule/Winter Solstice card relates to that pivotal moment that changes descent into ascent. In a spiritual sense this is the inner awakening and the realization that you have the power of renewal. The message of this card is that when it seems darkest in our lives, a new light begins to arise from deep within us. This is the light of the soul that cannot be extinguished because it is part of the divine light itself, which nothing can destroy.

For inner connections, see these cards: Priestess and Priest; Great Rite; all seasonal festivals/Sabbats.

Imbolc

DIVINATION MEANING

When this card appears, it seems as though things are frozen or stagnant, but forces must be brought to bear now that will break, release, or free the situation. You must find motivation. Purification comes from lighting the fires that will bring about change.

Keywords

Purification, Preparation, Anticipation.

TEACHING

Imbolc is the time of purification and preparation. The God is bound within the frozen land, awaiting release. The Goddess bears the fire of the smith that can transform substances, and thereby free the world from winter's grasp.

The card depicts the ritual setting for the Imbolc festival. Statues of the Goddess and God appear behind an altar, with the starry sky of night (for this is the Imbolc eve celebration). Here they stand as the Lady of Fire and the Lord of Ice.

IMBOLC

On the head of the Goddess is an ivy crown with nine white candles—nine is the mystical number of the Moon Goddess. The statue is decorated with the red, black, and white woven cords of the mystery tradition. Red represents the living blood of our ancestors, which flows in our veins. Black represents the deep shadows that contain the enlightenment awaiting the true seeker. White symbolizes what remains behind, a metaphor of the bone representing the wisdom and knowledge left behind by our ancestors.

Dangling from the cords tied to the Goddess are several reed objects known as Brid's crosses. These represent the union of the fertile male and female energies. On her statue crystal shards and white crocus appear, in honor of the Goddess's role in the solar season of the Wheel. In her hand the Goddess holds a white crocus flower. At her feet is a cauldron with glowing embers that will kindle the awakening fire to herald the coming of spring.

A lighted candle sits on the God statue, representing his divine presence, and there are icicles on his antlers.

Between the statues, the altar bears an ice block containing the frozen fire of the sun god. It is flanked by two candles representing the polarities and opposing forces of nature. The ice and fire rest on a bed of reeds, which play a role throughout the year as the God's cradle and his tomb.

THE SHADOW'S EDGE

The Imbolc card tells of liberation from bondage, inertia, or stagnation. The message of this card is that when all seems restricted and confined we must look to the inner fire of our passions. The card's imagery calls upon us to remember what motivates and drives us; why do we do what we do? When we remember what originally inspired us we can return empowered to fulfill our dreams.

For inner connections, see these cards: Tree in Winter; all seasonal festivals/Sabbats.

Tree in Spring

DIVINATION MEANING

When this card appears, things are ready to be renewed, new life is budding, and new vitality awakens.

Keywords

Renewal, Regrowth, Return.

TEACHING

The Tree in Spring symbolizes renewal and potential. It tells us that life follows death, and all things renew and return. In the spring we find that the promise of new life given at the winter solstice has now begun to manifest. A tree in spring does not dread the work ahead that will produce its buds, leaves, and flowers. It stands as a tree in spring, embracing what is natural to the conditions surrounding it while it awaits the ensured fullness of the coming summer.

The card depicts the arrival of spring with a tree in bud, and patches of the winter's snow are fading on the ground. New life springs forth from the soil.

TREE IN SPRING

THE SHADOW'S EDGE

The Tree in Spring card addresses the theme of renewal as an unending cycle. It is the fulfilled promise of return. In a spiritual sense the imagery speaks to us of the end of decline and the marked beginning of gain and prosperity. It is the soul in a new body with a new life experience ahead. For the soul this is the needed new vitality with which it can move forward again, refreshed, renewed, and ready to receive the new lessons that wait.

For inner connections, see these cards: Imbolc; Beltane.

Ostara/Spring Equinox

DIVINATION MEANING

When this card appears, it is time to create a strong vision, and plant the seeds of the harvest you desire. Much work is ahead, but your goal can be achieved.

Keywords

Planning, Plowing, Planting.

TEACHING

Ostara is the time of tilling the soil and planting the seeds. The Goddess has returned from the Underworld and is rejoined with the God. This is the divine couple whose union will make the world abundant with life.

The card depicts the ritual setting of the Ostara festival, which is marked by the spring equinox. Statues of the Goddess and God appear behind an altar, with the sun rising in the daytime sky. Here they stand as the Lady of the Lake and the Lord of the Reeds.

The statue of the God is decorated with the red, black, and white woven cords of the mystery tradition. Red represents the living blood of our ancestors, which flows in our

OSTARA/SPRING EQUINOX

veins. Black represents the deep shadows that contain the enlightenment awaiting the true seeker. White symbolizes what remains behind, a metaphor of the bone, representing the wisdom and knowledge left behind by our ancestors.

An antler is set on the God's statue, along with an eagle feather. Dangling from the cords are several bundles of plants with seed heads. On the horizon emerges a stag, representing the beginning of the agricultural year of growth and gain.

The Goddess statue holds a lighted candle, which symbolizes her divine presence. At her feet is a cauldron from which rises a magical mist that renews the earth, which has slept in the cold embrace of winter.

Between the statues on the altar sits a vase of narrowleaf cattails. It is flanked by two green candles representing the fertile polarities and forces of nature. Placed upon the altar are colored eggs, along with acorns and shells, which are ancient fertility symbols associated with this season.

THE SHADOW'S EDGE

The Ostara/Spring Equinox card relates to themes of fertility. In a spiritual sense this season is about the seed of creativity that gives birth to new visions. Ostara also promotes the prosperity of the inner light, which shines to guide our path ahead. In this way we bring growth and vitality to the experiences of our lives.

For inner connections, see these cards: Tree in Spring; all seasonal festivals/Sabbats.

Beltane

DIVINATION MEANING

When this card appears, it signifies a time to "let the magic work" and to let go of trying to control the situation. It can also indicate romance or a chance meeting that results in something special.

Keywords

Fertility, Union, Bonding.

TEACHING

Beltane is the time of fertility and union. In the myths and legends of some traditions the Goddess and God begin their courtship on May 1.

The card depicts the festival setting for the Beltane ritual. Statues of the Goddess and God appear behind an altar, with the starry sky of night in the background (for traditionally this is a May Eve celebration). Here they stand as the Lady of the Green and the Lord of the Green.

On the head of the Goddess is a crown of morning glory, primroses, and violets. The statue is decorated with the red, black, and white woven cords of the mystery tradi-

BELTANE

tion. Red represents the living blood of our ancestors, which flows in our veins. Black represents the deep shadows that contain the enlightenment awaiting the true seeker. White symbolizes what remains behind, a metaphor of the bone, representing the wisdom and knowledge left behind by our ancestors.

Dangling from the cords are white and red rose buds, which represent the joining of form and passion. On the statue of the Goddess appear shells and phallic symbols, representing the union of feminine and masculine. In her hand the Goddess holds a blossom, and all about her are fireflies in the night. At her feet is a cauldron filled with flower blossoms. In front of the cauldron appears the fallen antler of the God, symbolizing the passing of his reign into her hands, for the Goddess reigns from Beltane to Samhain (as the God reigns from Samhain to Beltane).

A lighted candle sits on the God statue, representing his divine presence.

Between the statues the altar is adorned with flowers placed on a bed of ivy, which represents the binding of the Goddess and God to one another. It is flanked by two red candles representing the passionate polarities and forces of nature. In the foreground lies a wand, representing the fertility of the season.

THE SHADOW'S EDGE

The Beltane card is about the principle of attracting elements that can join together for a greater purpose and function. The season specifically relates to the polarity of feminine and masculine (whether mundane or spiritual).

It is through bringing the polarities into harmony that the creative process and the ability to manifest something becomes possible.

For inner connections, see these cards: Great Rite; Priest and Priestess; Drawing Down the Moon; all seasonal festivals/ Sabbats.

Tree in Summer

DIVINATION MEANING

When this card appears, it indicates fullness, completion, abundance, a harvest to be realized.

Keywords

Fulfillment, Contentment, Assurance.

TEACHING

The Tree in Summer symbolizes the ripeness of maturity and abundance, and tells us to enjoy and appreciate the fruits of our labor. A tree in summer does not cling to the achievement of its goal. It stands as a tree in summer, embracing what is natural to the conditions surrounding it while it prepares to release its gains to the coming fall season.

The card depicts the fullness of summer with a tree filled with lush foliage. A stag approaches, symbolizing the virility and power of the season of growth.

TREE IN SUMMER

THE SHADOW'S EDGE

The Tree in Summer card speaks to us of the richness and fullness that comes from the joining of vital components. In nature it is the fruitfulness of plants and the fertility of herds. In the spiritual sense it is the joining of the feminine and masculine polarities into one consciousness, through which manifestation is birthed.

For inner connections, see these cards: Great Rite; Priestess and Priest; Drawing Down the Moon; Litha.

Litha/Summer Solstice

DIVINATION MEANING

When this card appears, it signifies that existing bonds endure, the light triumphs. Stand together and success is ensured. It can also mean not to forget to celebrate your achievements.

Keywords

Fullness, Unity, Harmony.

TEACHING

Litha is the time of acknowledging the fullness of the season. The Goddess and God are wedded as the divine couple of nature.

The card depicts the ritual setting for the Litha festival, which is marked by the summer solstice. Statues of the Goddess and God appear behind an altar, with the sun at its zenith above in the daytime sky. Here they stand as the Lady of the Flowers and the Lord of the Woods.

The statue of the God and Goddess are bound by the intertwined red, black, and white woven cords of the mystery tradition. Red represents the living blood of our ancestors

LITHA/SUMMER SOLSTICE

that flows in our veins. Black represents the deep shadows that contain the enlightenment awaiting the true seeker. White symbolizes what remains behind, a metaphor of the bone, representing the wisdom and knowledge left behind by our ancestors.

In the center appear a pair of mandrake roots with red and white roses, tied together to symbolize the union of the mated couple. Like the sun and the moon, which reside in the Underworld and rise daily to journey across the world of mortal kind, the mandrakes are symbols of the mystical Otherworld journey.

The antlers of the God hold oak leaves and acorns, re-minders of his fertile woodland nature. On his statue is an array of mistletoe, representing his mystical nature as Lord of Life and Death.

The Goddess statue holds a lighted candle, symbolizing her divine presence. She wears a crown of vervain blossoms, denoting her connection to the Faery realm. At her feet is a cauldron filled with sprouted grain, which symbolizes the seed of the God contained within her womb.

Between the statues the altar is set with a wedding cake indicating the divine marriage. It is flanked by two green candles representing the balance of the fertile polarities and forces of nature. Placed upon the altar are two chalices that symbolize the sacred essence of the Goddess and God, from which both will deeply drink. Rose petals are strewn across the altar, symbolizing the divine love.

THE SHADOW'S EDGE

The Litha or Summer Solstice card addresses the concept of marriage, whether it is physical, mental, or spiritual. It is the union of the essence of creation with the substance of creation; conjoined, the two manifest whatever concept is channeled through them. This is, in a spiritual sense, the divine marriage or the Heiros Gamos. It is following the summer solstice that the waning year commences. The divine marriage of polarities at this time ensures that one season does not annihilate the other. Instead, each polarity shares an equal portion of the year.

For inner connections, see these cards: Great Rite; The Kindred; Tree in Summer; seasonal festivals/Sabbats.

Lughnasadh

DIVINATION MEANING

When this card appears, it indicates that the "fruits of your labor" are manifesting from the planting of the long-term goal. Preparation to obtain your harvest must now begin. It is not yet time to rest, but the work ahead ensures the realization of your plans.

Keywords

Anticipation, Receptivity, Outcome.

TEACHING

Lughnasadh signals the beginning of the harvest season in northern European festivals. This card depicts the ritual setting for the Lughnasadh festival as the time of the anticipation of the coming harvest. Statues of the Goddess and God appear behind an altar, with the half-lit moon in the starry sky of night (for this is the eve celebration). Here they stand as the Lady of the Fields and the Lord of the Barley.

The statue of the Goddess is decorated with the red, black, and white woven cords of the mystery tradition. Red represents the living blood of our ancestors, which flows in

LUGHNASADH

our veins. Black represents the deep shadows that contain the enlightenment awaiting the true seeker. White symbolizes what remains behind, a metaphor of the bone, representing the wisdom and knowledge left behind by our ancestors.

Dangling from the cords around the Goddess are moon-flowers. On her statue appear vervain, rue, lavender, and rosemary. In her hand the Goddess holds a sprig of lavender. At her feet is a cauldron filled with fruit, which represents the full ripeness of the womb of the Goddess. A lighted candle sits on the God statue, representing his divine presence.

Between the statues the altar is set with a cornucopia overflowing with the bounty of nature. It is flanked by two pale yellow candles representing the decline of light as the days grow shorter.

THE SHADOW'S EDGE

The Lughnasadh card conveys the concept of receptivity and expectation. In the spiritual sense, this is the idea of not only being the vessel for manifestation but also behaving as though the desired change has already come about. This is one of the keys to magic.

For inner connections,, see these cards: All seasonal festivals and Sabbats.

Tree in Fall

DIVINATION MEANING

When this card appears, it indicates the time to release what no longer works.

Keywords

Decline, Shedding, Release.

TEACHING

The Tree in Fall symbolizes decline and release, and tells us to shed that which no longer serves the greater good. A tree in fall does not lament waning and loss. It stands as a tree in fall, embracing what is natural to the conditions surrounding it while it strips away what cannot be sustained in the coming winter season.

The card depicts the liberation of fall with a tree casting off its foliage.

THE SHADOW'S EDGE

The Tree in Fall card takes up the idea of shedding that which no longer serves the successful continuation of our lives. The message of this card is that we must rid ourselves

TREE IN FALL

of things that drain our energy and resources or detract from our necessary goals. Holding on to things that no longer serve the common good is to risk future health, prosperity, and vitality.

For inner connections, see this card: Mabon.

Mabon/Autumn Equinox

DIVINATION MEANING

When this card appears the work is done, and the manifestation and realization of your plans is at hand. It is time to celebrate.

Keywords

Harvest, Completion, Fulfill.

TEACHING

Mabon is the time of harvesting the full yield of nature. What was planted at the spring equinox is now ripe and mature.

The card depicts the ritual setting for the Mabon festival, which is marked by the autumn equinox. Statues of the Goddess and God appear behind an altar, with the sun setting, casting shadows upon the ground. Here they stand as the Lady of the Harvest and the Lord of the Sheaf.

The God is decorated with the intertwined red, black, and white woven cords of the mystery tradition, from which hang the sacred silver and golden boughs. Red represents the living blood of our ancestors, which flows in our

MABON/AUTUMN EQUINOX

veins. Black represents the deep shadows that contain the enlightenment awaiting the true seeker. White symbolizes what remains behind, a metaphor of the bone, representing the wisdom and knowledge left behind by our ancestors.

On the God statue appear oak leaves and acorns, representing his divine woodland nature. The Goddess statue holds a lighted candle, which symbolizes her divine presence. At her feet is an empty cauldron with nine white shells set in front. The cauldron represents the gateway to the Underworld through which the Harvest Lord must pass. For from the Goddess does all life issue forth, and to her must all life return. The nine white shells symbolize her triformis nature as the three Fates, plus her three aspects as maiden, mother, and crone, plus her rulership over the three realms of the Overworld, Middleworld, and Underworld.

Between the statues, the altar is set with a reed basket filled with the sacred harvest cakes. The basket is now the tomb of the God (as it had once been his cradle at Yule) and bears the symbol of the sun. Apples, pumpkins, and acorns adorn the altar. The basket is flanked by two white candles representing pillars between which the portal to the Underworld or Otherworld is entered. At the time of Mabon the God dies and journeys to the Underworld, where he waits in the realm of Shadow for his rebirth at Yule.

Behind the altar stands an upright sickle, which represents the harvester. A raven, the messenger of the Otherworld, swoops downward to land upon the sickle. This marks the death of the Harvest Lord, who must willingly fall so that his seed will ensure the renewal of life.

THE SHADOW'S EDGE

The Mabon/Autumn Equinox card reveals the harvest we have reaped from what was sown in an earlier season. In a spiritual sense this is the measure of the soul's journey through life. It is here that we look at the state of our lives, our condition, and our relationships. The harvest is the time to look at what has been sacrificed and what has been gained.

For inner connections, see these cards: Tree in Fall; all seasonal festivals/Sabbats.

Samhain

DIVINATION MEANING

When this card appears, it indicates veils, shadowed things, and plans not realized. It can also indicate hidden forces at work, ancestral connections awakening, and occult energy at play.

Keywords

Veiled, Indistinct, Shadowy.

TEACHING

Samhain is the time when the gateway between the worlds opens and allows passage to and from the Otherworld. It is the time when ancestral spirits can return to the world of the living.

The card depicts the ritual setting for the Samhain festival. Statues of the Goddess and God appear behind an altar, with the full moon in the starry sky of night for this is the eve celebration. Here they stand as the Lady of Shadow and the Lord of Shadow.

The statue of the Goddess is decorated with the red, black, and white woven cords of the mystery tradition. Red

SAMHAIN

represents the living blood of our ancestors, which flows in our veins. Black represents the deep shadows that contain the enlightenment awaiting the true seeker. White symbolizes what remains behind, a metaphor of the bone, representing the wisdom and knowledge left behind by our ancestors.

From the cords hang herbs, a bone, and a key. The herbs represent the altering of consciousness (mystical vision). The bone is a symbol of the dead, the ancestral connection. The key represents the opening between the worlds at this mystical season of the year.

On the Goddess statue appear pomegranates, which are symbols of the Underworld and its inner secrets. In her hand the Goddess holds a single pomegranate. At her feet is a cauldron filled with the harvest of the fall season.

A lighted candle sits on the God statue, representing his divine presence.

Between the statues, the altar bears a skull with cross-bones, symbols of the slain harvest lord. On the skull burns a red candle that symbolizes the living blood of the ancestral connection. The skull represents ancestral knowledge and wisdom (in essence, what is left behind after death). It is flanked by two black candles representing the realm of death and of procreation. Placed upon the altar are the fall harvest items.

THE SHADOW'S EDGE

The Samhain card speaks of ancestral voices and wisdom from the other side of life. This is the parting of the veil between the worlds, the moment when the Otherworld and the mortal world overlap. In a metaphysical sense, it is the merging of the subconscious mind and the conscious mind. This joining awakens psychic awareness, which lends itself to visions and oracle abilities.

For inner connections, see these cards: The Kindred; Chthonic Roots; Faery Door; The Fates; Otherworld; Three Great Mysteries; all seasonal festivals/Sabbats.

Triformis

DIVINATION MEANING

When this card appears, it signifies that other aspects, levels, or elements are at play. The card advises us to look back to the beginning, access the present, and contemplate the future. The matter is not one thing by itself. Different aspects will show themselves, and each will require discernment.

Keywords

Complexity, Depth, Expansion.

TEACHING

Manifestation requires three individual points or elements, which are time, space, and energy. This is called the triangle of manifestation. In a religious or spiritual view the Goddess, from whom all things issue forth, is a triple goddess. In modern times she is called the Maiden, Mother, and Crone. One ancient example of the triformis concept appears in the Greek view of the Fates as three woman who weave the lives of mortal kind. Another example is the goddess Hecate, whom ancient writers such as Lucan refer to as a goddess with three aspects (Hecate, Diana, Persephone/Proserpina).

TRIFORMIS

The card depicts the Great Goddess manifesting from within the night sky. She appears as a single being, with three aspects appearing as individual faces. On the left is the Maiden, in the center is the Mother, and to the right is the Crone.

The Goddess wears a lunar circlet, which links the three natures into one entity. A serpent appears wrapped around her arm, which represents her Underworld nature. A key hangs from the other arm, symbolizing her role as the gatekeeper and revealer of the hidden mysteries.

THE SHADOW'S EDGE

The Triformis card reveals the mystical nature of the number three. It addresses triple aspects that emanate from a core principle, a pattern established by nature in the cycles of human life: birth, life, and death. These are the three great mysteries from which all other mysteries originate.

For inner connections, see these cards: The Fates; Three Great Realms; Three Great Mysteries.

Chthonic Roots

DIVINATION MEANING

When this card appears, it indicates that very deep levels have opened. A process has begun that will take you through darkness and into enlightenment. Things are not as they appear to be, and your quest is to let the desire to know take you further down the road. The card can also mean to trust your visions and intuition. A magical and spiritual transformation is at hand.

Keywords

Traverse, Trepidation, Sixth Sense.

TEACHING

Potent herbs that alter states of consciousness have a long tradition in the mystical arts. They have been used to align the mind and spirit to the realities of other realms or dimensions. These dimensions are experienced as the Underworld or Otherworld, beyond the realm of mortal kind. Many ancient potions contain substances from such plants as the foxglove, aconite, henbane, hemlock, and belladonna (or nightshade). These deadly plants, prepared in precise

CHTHONIC ROOTS

portions, have been used to bring one close to death so that they can pass easily into the realms that reside beyond the world of mortal kind. The resulting visions and perceptions can be enlightening, and the power of oracle ability may also be achieved. However, without knowing the precise portions and ingredients, such plants are likely to cause death. (Do not experiment with any of these poisonous plants!)

The card depicts a hideaway area with an old well, which in ancient myths and legends is often depicted as an entryway into the Otherworld. A cloth is spread out upon the ground in front of the well. On the cloth are the harvested roots of a mandrake, datura, and aconite plant. A harvest sickle also lies on the cloth. Traditionally, such roots are harvested at night when the moon is dark or full. Sunlight is to be avoided when working with chthonic herbs.

THE SHADOW'S EDGE

The Chthonic Roots card contains the concept of transformation through altered states of consciousness. The theme is one of roots within the dark places of procreation, and of still waters that run deep into the hidden realms below. The message of this card is that we must enter into the deep recesses of the mind and spirit in order to pierce the darkness and retrieve the hidden or lost light.

For inner connections, see these cards: Faery Door; Between the Worlds; Samhain; Astral Body; Art of Magic; Centers of Power; Three Great Mysteries; Mortar and Pestle.

Astral Body

DIVINATION MEANING

When this card appears, it signifies that normal methods and views are no longer applicable. New ways of seeing and operating are needed. Move now to a new vantage point.

Keywords

Discernment, Insight, Perception.

TEACHING

The human body possesses a spirit body or double-form, which is called the astral body (meaning "of the stars"). This is the body that appears in our dreams and experiences sensations and emotions. It is used by the soul or spirit to travel outside of the limitations of the physical form. Tradition states that a silvery cord attaches the physical body to the astral body. As long as the cord remains, then the soul continues to be attached to the material form. At death the cord dissolves away and frees the soul to leave the world of mortal kind.

The card depicts a man sitting in a circle of stones as he enters into a trance. From his forehead emanates a silvery

ASTRAL BODY

cord that connects to his astral form, which flies off into the starry night sky. The soul journeys to the Otherworld nightly to enrich its education, for knowledge and experience of both realms are required in order for the soul to reach maturity.

THE SHADOW'S EDGE

The Astral Body card speaks to us of projected consciousness. Its message is that we do not require a material form in order to continue to exist. It is a reminder that the physical body is a temporary vessel animated by the soul. Therefore we must place as much emphasis on our spiritual lives as we do our material existence. To fail to do so is to live only half a life.

For inner connections, see these cards: Sacred Bough; Faery Door; Between the Worlds; Otherworld; Chthonic Roots; Centers of Power; Three Great Realms; Three Great Mysteries.

The Fates

DIVINATION MEANING

When this card appears, it indicates a situation or outcome that originates in a higher source. There are influences that you have no control over. However, the blessings of light and dark are at work around and within you. No doubt the Universe is unfolding as designed. No matter what your situation is, always remember that the Universe has no designs for your destruction, it operates only for your successful spiritual evolution.

Keywords

Fortune, Grand Design, Destiny.

TEACHING

Ancient myths and legends tell of the Fates, who are often depicted as three sisters. They are typically associated with weaving, and in their legends they weave the pattern of life for each human. One sister is a young maiden, another is a mature woman, and the third is elderly. This is an early form of the triple nature associated with the feminine forces

THE FATES

in the ancient mystery tradition. In ancient times the Fates were held to be greater than the Olympic gods.

The card depicts three hands, of varying age, around a spinning wheel. One hand holds the spindle, one hand turns the wheel, and another hand cuts the cord. The cut signifies the end of physical life, while the other hands symbolize the shades of light and dark that color our lives.

THE SHADOW'S EDGE

The Fates card reflects the triformis nature as a process, intimately connected to the cycles of life as a pattern. Its specific purpose reveals itself in the metaphysical teaching of the soul contract. This teaching tells us the soul enters into material life with a specific purpose, and that key events are predestined in life. However, the soul possesses free will, which can be used as desired by the soul. This can undo portions of the destiny pattern, and can even unravel sections. But ultimately the Fates bring closure and the soul is released.

For inner connections, see these cards: Triformis; Karma; Three Great Mysteries.

Karma

DIVINATION MEANING

When this card appears; it signifies you are at the meeting point of cause and effect. Your choices and actions, or lack thereof, have delivered this outcome. The choice is now before you, and you must accept responsibility and do what you inwardly know is right.

Keywords

Recompense, Response, Contagion.

TEACHING

Every act creates an energy that attaches itself to the person performing the act. This energy attracts whatever is harmonious with its vibration. Whether the energy is constructive or destructive, the return of energy matches it. This positive or negative energy is often carried by the soul into other lifetimes. This brings events and circumstances to each lifetime that strengthen or challenge the soul. Karma does not reward or punish; it simply aligns and matches energy. The results of this action are in the hands of the soul and the Source from which it came.

KARMA

The card depicts an entity in space who is displaying a scroll that bears a record of past deeds and future needs. In one hand he holds a crystal ball in which a glimpse of the future is possible. According to the teaching, the soul enters into a soul contract each lifetime, through which it eliminates negative karma through corrective actions and draws positive karma as a means of spiritual evolution.

THE SHADOW'S EDGE

The Karma card speaks to us of balance restored. The teaching centers on the belief that the soul attaches energy to itself throughout each life experience. It is not the actions that adhere to the soul; it is the feelings we hold in relationship to our experiences. Whatever we hold on to is the energy we create in the aura, which in turns attracts karma. Karma draws the soul into a situation through which the unbalanced energies that are detrimental to spiritual evolution can be dissolved. This is the fire of liberation that frees the soul.

For inner connections, see these cards: The Watchers; The Fates; Oath; Three Great Mysteries.

The Watchers

DIVINATION MEANING

When this card appears, it indicates the awakening of a new personal vision and an understanding of your place in the cosmos. You are not alone in this and guidance is available; however, direction is subtle and requires deep attention to the inner voice. The card can also indicate that something is about to be revealed, or that others are already aware without your knowledge.

Keywords

Observation, Witness, Reveal.

TEACHING

A race of beings exists who were once physical beings. These ancient beings have evolved into a spiritual race that watches over the gateways that connect all realms. In ancient times they were associated with specific stars, and the stars themselves were thought to be the eyes of the watchers in the night sky.

In many traditions the Watchers are associated with the four compass directions of north, east, south, and west. They

THE WATCHERS

are also associated with the four elements of earth, air, fire, and water. A common practice is to evoke or summon the Watchers to guard the ritual circle. Here they are called to each quarter, and different traditions use various names and methods to call the Watchers.

The card depicts the starry heavens with four distinct nebula clouds. Each cloud has a bright star glowing within it. A closer examination reveals four beings taking form within the nebula, the combined formation suggestive of a robed figure. Each of the four stars represents the ancient star associated with a specific Watcher. The Star Aldebaran, when it marked the vernal equinox, held the position of Watcher of the East. Regulus, marking the summer solstice, was Watcher of the South. Antares, marking the autumn equinox, was Watcher of the West. Fomalhaut, marking the winter solstice, was Watcher of the North.

THE SHADOW'S EDGE

The Watchers card presents the concept of divine memory. The theme of this card centers on the divine consciousness and its awareness of humankind, as well as its interaction in the life patterns of the soul as it travels through many lifetimes. The message of this card is that all things are remembered, and nothing is ever lost. The material and spiritual life should be lived with this in mind.

For inner connections, see these cards: Karma; Oath.

Art of Magic

DIVINATION MEANING

When this card appears, it indicates skill and knowledge, which comes from many sources connected to the practitioner of the arts. The card reminds us to draw upon our resources, both inner and outer.

Keywords

Interaction, Emersion, Mastery.

TEACHING

Traditionally, the magical arts were taught over many years and required personal application and effort. Tools were created as an aid to learning how to attract and direct magical energy. Ritual and magical tools are a means of connecting and interfacing, as well as wielding the forces to which we have access. They serve as a means of touching what is essentially untouchable.

ART OF MAGIC

The card depicts magical items and tools on a desk, along with an old grimoire containing spells and rituals. A black cat, symbolizing the mysteries that reside in the shadows, sits amidst the magical items. Behind the cat is the grimoire of ritual and magic, which contains all that is worthy of preservation. The pentacle, wand, athame, and chalice represent the interplay of the four elements of earth, air, fire, and water. On the desk are several papers containing symbols, which serve to encapsulate vital and important concepts. By looking at the symbols, the mind is directly linked to the energy that is connected to the thing it represents.

THE SHADOW'S EDGE

The Art of Magic card takes up the idea that reality can be reshaped and redirected by mystical means. The card reveals that tools and concepts exist that we may draw upon. These are the time-proven methods of those who came before us. The message of this card is that we can tap into the momentum of the past, a living current of ancestral energy flowing through time.

For inner connections, see these cards: Between the Worlds; Centers of Power; Drawing Down the Moon; Chthonic Roots; Mortar and Pestle.

Centers of Power

DIVINATION MEANING

When this card appears, it indicates the need to apply all that you have earned through training and developed through your life experience. This is a card of awakening and self-empowerment. Be confident and go with what you sense and feel.

Keywords
Skill, Confidence, Experience.

TEACHING

There are centers within the human body that draw, amplify, store, and project energy. Traditions vary as to how many centers there are, where they reside, and what purpose they serve. In the oldest teachings in European traditions there are three centers: forehead, solar plexus, and genital region. The forehead interfaces with divine forces, the solar plexus with spiritual forces, and the genitals with pure vital energy.

In eastern mysticism there are seven centers: crown, forehead, throat, heart, solar plexus, abdomen, and genital

CENTERS OF POWER

region. The crown is linked to the divine and the forehead is associated with psychic abilities. The throat is aligned to communication, and the heart is the seat of love vibrations. The solar plexus is the zone through which etheric energy that feeds the soul is absorbed. The abdomen is the zone of personal power, and the genitals are the region of vital forces that maintain health in the body.

The card depicts a man kneeling before a magical book from which vaporous energies arise. Each enters the man's body at different points and activates an inner center. Through this experience he is vitalized and attuned to greater forces outside that join with those within.

THE SHADOW'S EDGE

The Centers of Power card reveals that we possess connective points within our being, through which we can interface with other dimensions and with the divine source itself. The message of this card is to develop those centers so that our experience through interfacing with other realities is rich and complete.

For inner connections, see these cards: Art of Magic; Three Great Realms; Drawing Down the Moon; Elder Staff.

Elder Staff

DIVINATION MEANING

When this card appears, it indicates that you have reached a position in which you can offer guidance or direction to others. It can also indicate a need to move on in some manner, in order to serve a greater community or worthy cause.

Keywords

Teacher, Emissary, Director.

TEACHING

In ancient times, trees were worshipped or venerated. Among some tribes it was believed that trees were the dwelling place of a god or goddess. This is one reason why sacred groves were established. A branch was taken from the tree and carried by the priestess or priest as a sign of his or her connection with the deity of the grove. Traditionally, the branch measured the height of the person plus the length from the elbow to the end of the middle finger. The height represented personal rapport with the deity of the grove. The bend of the arm, and therefore its extension outward, symbolized that the elder was to reach out to those whom

ELDER STAFF

he or she encountered. Together these were the full measure of the elder. With staff in hand, the priestess or priest went out to the people as an emissary of their deity.

The card depicts a robed figure carrying a staff, which symbolizes his or her connection to the deity of the sacred grove. The full moon, an ancient symbol of the mystery tradition, shines in the night sky as it sheds light upon the path. This represents the inner mystery that light is at home in the darkness, and that enlightenment is found in passing through the night.

THE SHADOW'S EDGE

The Elder Staff informs us that the path we walk takes us through worlds not known by the average person in life. The light of the moon and stars guides the soul in different ways than does the light of the sun. The subtlety of their emanations is alluring, and their seeming aloofness draws us on to vistas of worlds unknown. The message of this card is to live and walk the chosen path with lasting devotion.

For inner connections, see these cards: Art of Magic; Sacred Bough; The Kindred; Otherworld; Priestess and Priest; The Watchers; Centers of Power; Three Great Realms; Mortar and Pestle; Perfect Love and Perfect Trust; Oath; Karma.

Sacred Grotto

DIVINATION MEANING

When this card appears, it indicates the closing of a rite of passage or personal journey, which now leads to a new cycle or chapter in one's life. It can also mean a return, but one in which the roles, conditions, and relationships have changed and must be honored.

Keywords

Gateway, Inner Direction, Mystical Vision.

TEACHING

The grotto is among the earliest sites of worship and veneration in ancient times. It is particularly associated with goddess worship and female mysteries. Fire was the primary symbol of the goddess at the grotto, and this evolved into such cults as that of Hestia or Vesta.

The card depicts the opening of a cave with a lighted torch blazing inside. A primitive altar sits outside with conch shells, ancient symbols of the feminine in goddess worship. Water flows, forming a crossroads, for this is the mystical water of the moon flowing from the Underworld/

SACRED GROTTO

Otherworld. Reeds, symbols of the god, arise in the marsh surroundings. This cave leads from the Otherworld back into the realm of mortal kind.

THE SHADOW'S EDGE

The Sacred Grotto card takes up the concept of divinity without personification. It is the pure and primal consciousness revealed in flame. The cave is the place of entering in, and it is the sanctuary. This theme conveys the ancient teachings of womb and transformation, and what flows from this principle. The message of this card is to not lose sight of what is primal and primary behind the images we create. We honor and venerate the principles and not the forms that express them.

For inner connections, see these cards: Sacred Site; Triformis; Otherworld; Between the Worlds.

Three Great Realms

DIVINATION MEANING

When this card appears, it indicates the reality of other dimensions that are not evident to one who sees only the surface or what is apparent or in plain view. The card reveals that there is more depth and a greater connection than what seems apparent in the situation.

Keywords

Expansive, Encompassing, Elaborate.

TEACHING

There are three realms that comprise the Universe. These are known as the Overworld, Middleworld, and Underworld. The Overworld contains the stars and the heavenly worlds. The Middleworld is the realm of mortal kind. The Underworld is the realm of the dead, and also contains the Otherworld of myth and legend.

In one of the earliest writings to mention the Three Realms (Hesiod's *Theogony*), we find that the goddess Hecate reigns over the three known realms of the ancient world. Hecate, in her earliest reference, is depicted as a

THREE GREAT REALMS

great goddess who grants fertility, victory, and good fortune. In later times we find the introduction of elements that associate her with the dead and the crossroads, and portray her as a crone figure.

In the mystical tradition of the broom, we find it made of an ash handle, a birch brush, and willow straps that bind it all together. In old lore associated with the broom, it is used for magical flight, and is therefore connected to the Three Great Realms as a vehicle for traversing the worlds.

The card depicts a Book of Shadows opened to a page portraying a broom-like tree that represents the three worlds. Its branches reach into the sky where birds, the messengers of the gods, come to nest. Its roots twist and move downward like serpents into the dark secrets that reside in the shadowy Underworld.

In many old legends we find tales of the World Tree symbolizing the structure and supporting system of the Universe. In some myths we find the tree as a symbol of enlightenment, such as in the tale of Odin, who hangs suspended from a tree until he gains enlightenment.

The tree is, in essence, a bridge that unites the Three Great Realms. In the Middleworld of mortal kind, the tree is often shown with a hollow in the center, which is known as a faery door. Through the gateway located in the Middleworld, one can enter and exist in the other dimensions beyond. However, the way is open only to those who have the courage and fortitude to explore the mysteries within and without.

THE SHADOW'S EDGE

The Three Great Realms card speaks to the three levels through which we connect to other realities. In a spiritual sense it also reflects the three parts of the soul: the higher self, middle self, and lower self. This spiritual design establishes a transitory state that allows the soul to explore and integrate all levels of its consciousness and its experiences along the path of evolution. The message of this card is to not be bound to any sense of weakness, but to honor personal achievements as well as failures with an eye towards what is ideal and beneficial for the future.

For inner connections, see these cards: Centers of Power; Faery Door; Otherworld; Oak, Ash and Thorn; The Watchers; Astral Body; Triformis.

Three Great Mysteries

DIVINATION MEANING

When this card appears, it indicates a life passage related to birth, life, or death. Some significant event is unfolding, which will create profound changes in your life and your relationships with others.

Keywords

Cycles, Exploration, Culmination.

TEACHING

The Three Great Mysteries are birth, life, and death. In essence these ask the questions: where did we come from, what are we doing here, and what happens to us when we die? In ancient times the Fates were believed to rule over life, and were depicted as three women: a young woman, a mature woman, and an elderly woman. In art they are portrayed at a weaving loom, working with the threads of life. At the end, the elderly woman cuts the thread, which ends the life of the person whose life-pattern was woven.

The Three Great Mysteries are sometimes referred to as the Wheel of Life, which is a teaching connected to reincarnation. In this view the soul enters into a new physical

THREE GREAT MYSTERIES

body, through which it learns valuable lessons as it works toward spiritual evolution. After many lives the soul obtains release from having to return to the material world. At this point it enters into life within the spiritual realms that exist beyond the world of mortal kind.

One associated teaching portrays souls as traveling through time and space together, bound by karmic energies that reunite various souls in a variety of relationships. In this scenario, parents and children may trade places in various lives. This also hold true for gender roles in love relationships. One very old teaching maintains that magical ties bring souls back into the same family lines. Such teachings indicate hereditary families of magical or witchcraft lineage.

The Three Great Mysteries card depicts a Book of Shadows opened to a page. On this page are the three symbols of the mysteries: the seed, a ripened plant, and the harvest sickle. These represent the agricultural mysteries wherein the seed is the struggle for survival, the plant is the fullness of life experience, and the sickle is the return of seed, and life, back into the soil. This is associated with the old belief that from the womb of the goddess all life issues forth, and to her must all life return.

THE SHADOW'S EDGE

The Three Great Mysteries card takes up the idea of reincarnation: the process and the portals through which the soul enters, experiences, and then leaves material existence. The message of this card is that our lives have purpose and meaning, but that this lies in something greater than ourselves.

The clues are veiled from the soul by material birth; where did we come from? They are bypassed by the distractions of material existence; why are we here? The final clue is diverted by the thoughts of eventual death; where do we go from here? The answer resides not in what is the meaning of life, but in what is the purpose of existence itself.

For inner connections, see these cards: The Fates; Ostara; Litha; Mabon.

Charge of the Goddess

DIVINATION MEANING

When this card appears, it indicates that what is sought or desired is not found in the outside world but resides instead within the inner self. The card encourages intuitive feeling as a guide, and speaks of trusting our connection to the divine.

Keywords

Inner Truth, Introspection, Revelation.

TEACHING

The Charge of the Goddess addresses one of the great mystical truths, which states that fulfillment lies within the soul's attainment and not within the achievements of the body or personality it inhabits. The teaching states that within us is the connection to the Source of All Things. Through an inward journey we can interface with the source and discern the way that is most beneficial for our spiritual education and evolution.

The inward journey includes an acceptance and appreciation of the divine spark within, for each of us is the offspring

CHARGE OF THE GODDESS

of that which created the Universe. One of the keys we need to embrace is the understanding that we must be an open vessel into which the Universe can pour the fulfillment of our needs and desires. The Universe matches energy for energy. It is therefore vital to draw what you desire and avoid what you do not want in your life. The Universe is listening. What are your thoughts, feelings, and actions asking the Universe to send you?

The card depicts an open Book of Shadows that is turned to the page containing the mystery text of the Charge. The circlet of a High Priestess rests on the corner of the book. Around the border of the page appear moonflowers and the starry heavens, which represent the blossoming of divine enlightenment. The sacred text reveals the keys to unlock the inner mystery.

THE SHADOW'S EDGE

The Charge of the Goddess card speaks to us of the higher nature, which is the calling of the divine source to the spark that is its progeny. The message of this card is that we come as souls into material life with the inner awareness necessary for discernment. At the core of our being is the spark that was born from the source of creation itself. In order to unravel the mysteries, we need only interface with the source through the center of our being—for if we cannot feel the inner guidance, and sense the truth deep within us, then there is nothing in the external world that can truly lead us in ways that are valuable.

For inner connections, see these cards: Otherworld; Drawing Down the Moon; Triformis; Astral Body; Centers of Power; Elder Staff; Sacred Grotto.

Mortar and Pestle

DIVINATION MEANING

When this card appears, it indicates integration, the combining of separate elements into a single substance. The card also indicates refinement.

Keywords

Integration, Incorporation, Merging.

TEACHING

The integration and blending of various plant and mineral substances has long been part of the magical and mystical tradition. This is, in essence, the alchemical formula. The mortar represents the feminine womb and the pestle symbolizes the masculine phallus. Here is the point of limitless potential.

The card depicts a mortar and pestle sitting on a work table, surrounded with herbs and potion vials. A plant rests in the mortar, awaiting transformation and integration.

MORTAR AND PESTLE

THE SHADOW'S EDGE

The Mortar and Pestle card reflects the concept of refinement and integration. This is the internal process of the mysteries. We must study the ancestral heritage and glean the gems of wisdom that are covered in mystical concepts, myths, and legends. Then we can separate the chaff from the grain, keep what is worth keeping, and with a breath of kindness blow the rest away.

For inner connections, see these cards: Chthonic Roots; Great Rite.

Perfect Love
and Perfect Trust

DIVINATION MEANING

When this card appears, it indicates a common goal or outcome that is shared by kindred spirits in a single vision (void of personal gain, jealousy, or greed).

Keywords

Trust, Loyalty, Fidelity.

TEACHING

The concept of perfect love and perfect trust is rooted in the idea of shared vision and mutual goals and intentions. The theme of perfection is related to coming together in sacred space to venerate the Goddess and God. Here love can be experienced beyond human understanding. Trust is rooted in the knowledge that no ill will exists, and that the needs of one person are equal to the needs of all in attendance.

PERFECT LOVE AND PERFECT TRUST

THE SHADOW'S EDGE

The Perfect Love and Perfect Trust card conveys our connection with the great design. It is from the union of the soul with the creative source of its origin that we emanate the light that arises from such a blending. In this light one can only walk in accord with the balance and harmony of that which gives equilibrium to the universe (the source itself). This is the perfect trust of the soul in the perfect love of its creator. Once fully joined with this principle, the soul can radiate this to others in the community of souls.

For inner connections, see these cards: Charge of the Goddess; Oath; Priestess and Priest; Great Rite; Drawing Down the Moon; Centers of Power.

Oath

DIVINATION MEANING

When this card appears, it indicates that "your word is your bond," and its meaning is to keep your word and to be true and authentic to yourself.

Keywords
Truth, Trust, Integrity.

TEACHING

Oaths of initiation are common within any mystery tradition. Part of the traditional oath is to not reveal any of the practices of the system. The mandate is often to keep silent, and to not share any initiate teachings or materials with non-initiates of the specific system. This is typically marked by such words as "I swear this oath by the blood in my veins" and "by my honor among my brothers and sisters of the Art."

The card depicts a man with his hand over his face. The tips of his middle and index fingers are beneath his eyes, forming a V shape. This gesture is known as "the witch's honor."

OATH

THE SHADOW'S EDGE

The Oath card reflects personal honor and loyalty. The oath is the token of the soul's integrity, given in community. The oath is the testimony of the inner self. The value of the oath is not in it being sworn. Instead, its value lies in it being trusted by the people who receive it. This means that the oath can be relied upon because of the integrity of the person who swears the oath. The message of this card is to be worthy of such trust by others.

For inner connections, see these cards: Perfect Love and Perfect Trust, Elder Staff, Karma, The Watchers.

Journey Through the Hidden Path

The following exercise is designed to serve two purposes. One is to help you recall the essential meaning of each card, and the other is to create mystical alignments between you and the spiritual keys contained within the card imagery. This is accomplished by reading the story in this section. This will take awhile, so make sure you are not rushed for time. It is very important not to skim read this section or jump around in the text.

To start, make sure the cards are in the exact order in which they appear in the table of contents. As you read the story, you will encounter the name of each card appearing inside a bracket [like this]. When you see this bracket, stop reading and place the named card in front of you. Study its teaching for a few moments and then continue reading the story again. Repeat this for each card. Let us begin.

[Sacred Bough] You are walking along a footpath that wanders through the grassy hills. Before you appears the crossroads, which lead off into two separate directions. In the center of the crossroads stands the sacred tree. Suspended from a branch is the sacred bough of ancient myth and legend. You have come to the beginning of a quest placed before you by the Fates. An important decision is now at hand.

A spirit voice whispers to you and tells you that you must take the sacred bough from the tree. With this in hand, you may pass safely into the Otherworld that lies beyond the world of mortal kind. As you gaze upon the tree you see a key tied to a colored cord. This is the symbol of the enterer, one who can pass through guarded gateways. Upon the tree is the sign of the goddess Hecate, a deity who escorts the traveler across the threshold into the Otherworld.

You reach out and take the sacred bough in your hand. Inwardly you know that your life will never be the same again, for you will see with clearer eyes when your journey has reached its end. You choose one of the roads leading off into the hills, and your walk has begun.

As you walk along the footpath, it leads deep into the woods. The path ends and you find yourself in front of a small hawthorn tree that seems to be blocking the way [Oak, Ash and Thorn]. A voice whispers to you, saying, "None may freely pass here before the time has come." You realize that you stand at the legendary meeting place of oak, ash, and thorn. Herein lays the hidden gateway to the great realm beyond. The thorns of the hawthorn appear formidable, and you instinctively hold the sacred bough in your hand out in front of you, feeling a sense of protection.

A sudden gust of wind rushes past you from behind, and the hawthorn branches part to allow it passage, for the guardian acknowledges your right to pass. You are welcomed in honor of the symbol you carry [Faery Door]. You look in amazement upon a wooden door that now appears between the ash and the oak tree. The sacred triple symbol is fixed in place on the door. The doorknob is shaped like an apple, which is sacred to the faery race. As you look at the door it begins to open, and a mystical light pours out through the crack of the door frame. You know you must pass through the door to whatever awaits you.

You gather your courage and pass through the doorway, as you still carry the sacred bough. The door closes behind you and you find yourself in a bright mist that obscures your sight. In a few moments the light dims and you begin to see shapes around you [Between the Worlds].

With your vision restored, you find yourself next to a river flowing off into the horizon. There is a dreamlike nature to the riverbank and trees. As you take in the view, four orbs of light float toward you. They hover by the river as they seem to study you. As you sense that these orbs are conscious beings, you also sense that in the water of the rushing river are the thoughts and desires of people in the mortal world being carried into the astral realm beyond the horizon. This is a place of the elements of creation, a realm between the worlds of thought and the forms that result from them in the material world.

The orbs begin to drift away in the direction of the horizon. The light in the distance draws you down along the banks of the river. As you reach the horizon you are once again engulfed in a bright mist, and your eyes are blinded by the light.

Standing motionless you hear beautiful music that sounds like soft bells mixed with the trickle of a gentle stream. The light surrounding you becomes pleasant and warm [The Kindred]. From out of the light emerge four figures, and as they draw close, you realize that these are Faery beings from the Otherworld. They look upon the sacred bough you carry, greet you, and bid you welcome. "We shall be your guides and guardians in places unknown to you," they say, and they gesture for you to follow them.

The Kindred speak with you and tell you they will take you to meet their Lord and Lady, who dwell on the white island of the mists. You follow them along the river until it flows into a beautiful lake. A boat rests upon the shore of the lake, and within it is a beautiful woman [Otherworld]. The Kindred tell you that this is the priestess of the Lady of the Lake, and they help you into another boat to follow as her boat slips off into the lake. As you look forward you can see that mist envelops the lake, keeping you from being able to view what lies beyond.

The priestess raises her arm and three swans appear overhead. She directs them into the mist, and as they fly, the movement of their wings begins to part the mysterious mist. As the mist opens you can see the white shores ahead, and beyond this a castle tower is glimpsed in the distance. You are entering the center of the Otherworld, the realm of the immortal ones.

After crossing the lake you are left at the shore with the kindred, who lead you down a path from the beach into the woods [Oak King]. Standing in the pathway is a man clad in woodland garb and holding a staff. The Kindred introduce you, saying that he is the Oak King. They inform you that they are now departing, and will see you again before your journey's end.

The Oak King leads you down the woodland path. He tells you that he is the spirit of all growing things, and that he restores the cycle of growth and gain. His story is ageless, and in his words you see visions of the primordial world. You feel the power and tenacity of Nature, a force that cannot be tamed nor terminated.

As you walk along the road, the Oak King points to a man standing further down the path. "This is my brother, the Holly King" he tells you, and then he instructs you to meet him down the road. As you look back, the Oak King is gone and you see only a great stag moving away, deep into the woods [Holly King].

The Holly King greets you as you approach. As you walk with him, the Holly King speaks of the need for decline so that the balance of Nature is preserved. He explains that death is the preparation for new life, that harshness provides the strength to rejuvenate, and how decay sustains growth. His story is ageless, and in his words you see visions of rich primal soil, deep roots, and ripe seeds waiting in the darkness of the earth.

The Holly King leads you down the path and points down the road, informing you that around the bend you will encounter an important sign. As you look back, the Holly King is gone, and you see only a gray wolf slipping off deep into the woods. The road lies ahead and you journey onward.

[Sacred Site] Before long you come to a great standing stone. The stone has stood upon this spot for countless ages. A large hole is worn through the upper part of the standing stone, and through this you see a stone circle by a tree in the distance. You realize this is the sign spoken of by the Holly King. The stone has narrowed your vision to a single point, and this is where your footsteps must now take you on your quest.

As you move toward the stone circle, the Kindred appear on the path. "It is time," they say. "And the hour of our meeting is here." You notice that a couple is now standing by the stone circle, and you are taken to meet them [Priest and Priestess]. As you approach, the couple extend their hands to welcome you. The Kindred explain that these are the priestess and priest of the Old Ways. Looking upon them. you realize that you are in the company of a Lord and Lady of the Faery realm. Behind them is a mystical sky, with the orbs of spirits moving within its astral fluid.

You follow the priestess and priest into the circle of stones and prepare yourself to pass through an initiation into the great hidden mysteries. You kneel in front of the priest and priestess as they hold the ritual tools. The priestess lifts her chalice and presents it to the priest. He raises his wand upward into the air. A purple mist, the color of the moon's magic, envelops you and obscures all sight.

Suddenly a vision unfolds within the mist. You see a man in front of you kneeling before a beautiful woman [Drawing Down the Moon]. The man forms his hands to create a triangle, through which he focuses upon the woman. She raises her arms and stands as if in a trance. Behind the woman you see an image forming. This is the divine presence of the Goddess of the Three Great Realms. She enters into the woman and the two become one, joined in matter and spirit.

The purple mist once again closes around you, and as it clears you can see the chalice and wand once again. In an instant the sky has changed to sunlight, and the priest lowers his wand down into the chalice of the priestess [Great Rite]. As the chalice and wand unite, you feel the world shift beneath you, and a cold wind blows across the circle of stones.

You look up and see that the tree near the stone circle is bare and covered with snow [Tree in Winter]. The priest speaks to you, saying, "Behold the tree in winter, the spirit of Nature that endures what is most harsh in life." A wolf passes by the tree and briefly pauses as he notes your presence. You realize that he is the agent of balance that governs life and death in this season of limited resources. You breathe in the cold air and become one with the season, and the balance, and the dance of life and death.

The priestess and priest motion you to follow them. You walk over the hill and down into an open area. Before you is an altar flanked by statues of the Goddess and God of the Old Ways [Yule]. The priest speaks again: "You have passed through the tree in winter, and before you now is the first hope of the return to warmth and abundance." Upon the altar you see a symbolic infant known as the Child of Promise. This is the sun in its infancy, nestled in a cradle of woven reeds. The sun rises on the horizon, and the birth of its rays causes the shadows to wash across the snow. Fire rises from the cauldron in front of the goddess statue, and you breathe in the warm air. The promise of the coming season is in you now.

The priestess steps forward and raises her arms upward. In response, the night takes the sky, and the stars look down upon the setting [Imbolc]. Upon the altar the fire of the sun is encased in ice, bound in the frozen season. Candles glow upon the crown of the goddess statue, symbolizing her passion that is the fire of the forge. "Before you," the priestess says, "is that which is bound and that which liberates." The ice glows upon the altar and its light emanates outward. It is cool as you breathe in its essence, but you feel warmth growing within you. Fire and ice embrace your inner spirit.

You look back at the priestess and priest, and they smile as they lift the chalice and wand. In unison, they say, "And the Wheel turns." Suddenly you are back at the tree, which is now in bud [Tree in Spring]. The snow remains as only small patches, and flowers have appeared around the tree. The priestess speaks: "Behold the tree in spring." A soft wind passes over you and as you breathe in, the scent of fresh greenery enters and fills you. The forces of renewal awaken in your spirit. You realize that return, renewal, and regrowth is assured, for such is the way of Nature.

The priestess and priest lead you back to the ritual setting [Ostara]. The priest raises his wand, and in response the sun takes the sky. A goddess-shaped vase of reeds sits upon the altar. The reeds push up from the opening as though being given birth. Vapor rises from the cauldron in front of the goddess statue. This is the magical water of the womb, and of the magical lake of the goddess. The priest speaks: "The primal marsh unites the reed and the water." You feel the damp vapor rising from the cauldron, and the air you breathe in is thick and moist. Timelessness fills you with the vital essence of fertility, the force from which the world was born.

The priestess steps forward and raises her chalice, and in response the starry night prevails [Beltane]. Upon the altar appear flowers with a seductive fragrance. Fireflies dance around the goddess statues in magical flight. An antler in front of the goddess glows with power, and the wand on the altar resonates the essence of virility. The scent of musk mixes with the fragrance of flowers, and as you breathe in the enchanted vapors you are charged with electrical and magnetic passion.

You take in a deep breath, feeling overwhelmed. The priestess and priest raise their magical tools, and in unison say, "And so the Wheel turns." Suddenly you are once again in front of the tree, which has reached its fullness [Tree in Summer]. The priest speaks: "Behold the tree in summer." A stag briefly pauses as it takes note of your presence. You realize that the stag is the force of growth and vitality that moves the world to completion. A summer breeze passes through the leaves, and you joyfully breathe in, deeply receiving the essence of abundance and harmony.

As before, you return to the ritual setting with the priestess and priest [Litha]. The priest raises his wand and the sun illuminates the sky. Upon the altar is a wedding cake and two chalices of union. The cords of handfasting unite the goddess and god statues. Here is reflected the joining of the two forces whose marriage brings abundance to the world of Nature. The fragrance of the wine floats past you, and you breathe in the essence of polarity in accord.

The priestess raises her chalice, and the half moon claims the night sky [Lughnasadh]. Upon the altar is a cornucopia filled with the fruits of Nature's bounty. This is the promise of the harvest to come. The cauldron in front of the goddess statue overflows with fruit and symbolizes the ripe and full womb of the goddess who is pregnant with the harvest. The scent of fruit and grain rises in the air, and you breathe in the promise of return and reward.

You turn to the priestess and priest, who again raise the chalice and wand. Within moments you stand before the tree once again. The priestess speaks: "Behold the tree in fall." The colored leaves of autumn flash their display of beauty. You sense that release is approaching and the tree will soon shed the fullness it reached in the summer season. The crisp air of the changing season drifts across you, and you breathe in the realization that change requires release, and the things that no longer serve must be released.

You return with the priestess and priest to the ritual setting, the priest raises his wand in the air. The light of a setting sun creates shadows that fall behind the statues. Upon the altar are the harvested goods of Nature. A sickle rises up from the altar, symbolizing the slaying of the Harvest Lord. A raven is landing on the sickle, a sign that the portal to the Underworld is opening. He flaps his wings three times and the air moves across your face. You breathe in lightly, and feel heaviness within your center. You hear an inner voice, and it is the raven speaking, "For the seed must willingly fall so that new life may rise."

The priestess steps forward and raises her chalice. The day gives way to night, and the full moon rises to lighten the darkness. Upon the altar you see a skull with crossbones. This is the ancestral gateway between the Otherworld and the world of mortal kind. A sudden breeze seems to come from the altar, leaves scatter, and you breathe in the essence of the mysteries themselves. Life and death, dark and light, positive and negative all come together as the two parts of the one whole.

The priestess and priest leave offerings at the altar and tell you to remain here. You watch the full moon as you wait. After a few moments the moon begins to blur, as though your eyes are growing tired. You rub your eyes and look again, seeing the moon appear as three overlapping disks. Suddenly they magically merge into a goddess-form in the night sky [Triformis].

Where the light of the moon had been you see a candle, which is held by the figure of the goddess in the heavens. She wears a dress of stars that form about her. As she looks down upon you, with each movement of her head you can see two other faces fade in and out. She is young, mature, and elderly, all within the same moment in time and space.

She speaks to you, saying, "Come to me all who seek that which is hidden, and unto you shall all things be revealed. But know that your seeking and yearning will avail you not, until you embrace the mystery. For if that which you seek is not found within you, you will never find it in the world." You pause for a moment and then you say, "I will come, and I shall find."

The light of the moon leads you down a pathway through the woods and up to a small hill [Chthonic Roots]. You see an enchanted well, with plants growing around it. On the ground is a cloth spread open, upon which several roots are lying with a sickle. These are the magical plants of the powers of night. You take the roots to the well, dip them in water, and then drink the drops falling from the roots.

The Kindred appear before you and lead you back to the stone circle. They instruct you to sit quietly, and they tell you that your inward journey has begun. You sit and wait, feeling yourself growing drowsy [Astral Body]. After a few moments you feel a tingling sensation emanating from your feet and moving up toward your head. You feel an acceleration and suddenly find your spirit rushing upward, leaving your body behind.

In the night sky you fly to the Triformis goddess. Where the full moon had been you see now an old spinning wheel [The Fates]. Three hands work the process, and you realize that here are the threads and patterns of your own life. All your words, thoughts, feelings, and deeds have formed a fabric of intricate designs. But it is not finished yet, for the last thread has yet to be cut.

As you gaze at the spinning wheel, it appears to suddenly drop, but you quickly realize that it is but a symbol on a large scroll that has unrolled before your eyes [Karma]. Here in space, hovering before you, is a hooded figure holding the open scroll in one hand and a crystal ball in the other.

You look at the hooded figure, and ask, "What words are written on this scroll?" The figure answers, "Each mark on this scroll was made by you, it is your story. Your spirit is the parchment and your mind and heart are the pen and ink. I do not know what is written here because it belongs to you. It is yours to carry, and it is your message."

You look at the crystal ball, and ask its purpose. The hooded figure replies, "This is the world you have yet to create. But it is not pure, for in it are reflected the markings on this scroll." The hooded figure hands you the scroll and says, "This is what is and what has been." You take the scroll, and the figure hands you the crystal ball, saying, "This is what yet can be."

You take the objects and hold them close. The hooded figure fades away into the darkness of the night sky, leaving only the stars behind. But you are not alone in this place [The Watchers]. The beauty of the night sky is beyond anything you have seen. Nebulas form amidst the galaxies, and you notice four brilliant stars shining brighter than all the rest. Mystical voices whisper in the deep places, and they speak, "We are the Watchers, and all that has been and all that is, do we hold the memory thereof." The coolness of space surrounds you as you peer at the stars before you. The Watchers continue, "We are entrusted with the truth, so that it is not lost to this view or that view, this side or that side. For truth is the first casualty of any conflict, and though both sides claim the truth, neither can see beyond their own perspective. We bear witness to all that has transpired."

You look down at the earth below you and see the circle of stones and the ritual area where the altar and statues stand. The Watchers come closer and speak again, "We are the Old Ones, guardians of the ways to and from. None pass without our notice, and none escape our witness. We have been among your ancestors since the days when oak and boulder taught them of Nature and of the gods. We are known by many names, and to some we are the Dread Lords of the Outer Spaces." You hear each Watcher whisper something in your ear, but the language is foreign and you do not understand the words. Before you can respond, the stars grow larger and then quickly collapse inward, disappearing amidst the vast array of twinkling lights.

A sudden tugging feeling pulls on you, and you feel yourself falling. Quickly you are back in your physical body within the stone circle. The priest and priestess stand with the Kindred, waiting for you to recover from your inner and outer journey. You have no words to describe your experience, and no one asks you to try.

The Kindred walk you over to the tree outside of the circle. Together they reach into a small hollow and magically spread it open, exposing a doorway. You enter a room within the tree and are seated before a table [Art of Magic]. "Here," explain the Kindred, "time as you understand it does not exist." You nod as though you understand. The Kindred smile at one another, and then begin to teach you about each object on the table. Four voices speak all at once, each voice faster and faster until the sound becomes like the hum of a large beehive.

The buzzing sound continues, and in front of you the hands of the Kindred move with lightning speed. Tools are lifted and manipulated, the magical book opens, and words lift off the page, turning into visual concepts. Everything spins, and hums, as a magical light contains it all in a single vision before your eyes. You have learned the arts of magic in the timelessness of the faery realm, a training that your mortal body would not have lived to complete.

The Kindred hand you the magical book and take you out through the hollow of the tree. The priest and priestess return and instruct you to kneel [Centers of Power]. The book is set in front of you and opened to a page with three symbols. The Kindred begin to hum like the sound of bees, and the priestess and priest speak an incantation. The book begins to glow, and magical vapors rise from the page of the book. The vapors form like magical serpents, and they rise, entering your body through the three centers that govern body, spirit, and mind. Each center within your body glows in response to the magical energy. Your training and elevation have been completed. The Kindred give you three herbs, saying, "When you know the Great Mystery, join these together as one." The Kindred then depart.

After allowing a rest, the priestess and priest present you with the magical book and take you into the sacred grove that surrounds the ritual setting of altar and statues. You arrive at the sacred tree of the grove, where you stand before its grandeur. Together the three of you select a branch from the sacred tree, which will serve as your staff. The proper measure is taken in accord with tradition, offerings are given, and the branch is cut from the tree. The priestess hands you a robe, and you put it on [Elder Staff]. It is time now to return from the Otherworld and go back to the realm of mortal kind. For you must return to your people and bring the mysteries into the mundane world. You slip the magical book into your robe, and with staff in hand your journey is before you.

You begin walking down the path alone; the stars seem to be watching you as your footsteps bring you homeward. The night is silent and the air is sweet with jasmine and wisteria. The trail leads you to a cave set in the marshes [Sacred Grotto]. You see an altar set with the conch shells, the ancient symbols of the goddess. Within the cave is a torch, blazing with the feral fire of the goddess. Through the caverns and tunnels of this cave is the way of return to the world of mortal kind.

You enter the cave and begin the long journey home. The flowing waters of the Underworld lead you in your return. You pass the pool of the moon, whose waters renew the earth each spring. Beyond is the soft glow of light coming in from the outside. You approach it and encounter a cave opening, which is the passageway into the world of the living. You cross through and pause to allow your eyes to adjust to the new light.

In the distance you see a cottage. This is the cottage of the crone, the legendary mediator between humankind and the Faery race. Your heart remembers this place well, for this was where it all began for you so many years ago. You cross the field and enter the cottage with a feeling of being home once again.

You sit at the old desk in the cottage. The old Book of Shadows still sits in the book stand as it had so long ago. You remove the magical book from your robe and place it on top of the Book of Shadows. Sitting back to relax, you notice that a glow is forming around the books. It grows brighter and the books begin to lose their physical form. They turn into astral replicas, and then the light begins to dim. To your amazement the books reform into one large single volume.

You lean forward to touch the book, but it suddenly opens itself [Three Great Realms]. A page marker is already in place, holding the writing quill that has scribed your story. You realize that this is the affirmation of your quest through the three realms, and that you have now completed your journey back to the crone's cottage. You look at the picture in the book and see the sacred broom-like tree that symbolizes the three great realms. You glance over to the corner of the room and smile as you note the crone's broom leaning against the wall. It is well-worn from traversing the worlds.

You hear the pages of the Book of Shadows turning, and as you look you see them stop at a page titled the Three Great Mysteries [Three Great Mysteries]. These you know well, for you have crossed from the world of mortal kind carrying the sacred bough. You have traversed the realms of the Otherworld, and have returned from the depths of the Underworld. For you the mystery is now knowledge turned to wisdom. You lean upon your elder staff with the peace of enlightenment and the unrest of responsibility.

Your thoughts drift back to the Otherworld, and you recall the ritual setting with the altar and statues of the goddess and god. You can still feel the presence of the priest and priestess who guided you through the Wheel of the Year. The sacredness of your journey unites your mind, heart and spirit into one sphere of harmony. You decide to step outside of the cottage and breathe some fresh air. Once outside you look back at the cave opening, and recall the fire of the goddess. You think of her fire as the forge of transformation, and as the fire of passion that frees the god from his frozen bondage in winter. It is then that you realize her torch is in the center of the cave, as the sun's fire is frozen in the center of the ice at Imbolc. The inner secret is the center, and its liberation is unity. The inner journey leads inward to the place where one can connect with that which unites the soul with the outer world.

You return to the desk in the cottage. Looking at the Book of Shadows you notice the pages have been turned again, and hung over the edge of the book is the circlet crown of a priestess. The open page reads: Charge of the Goddess [Charge of the Goddess]. The runic script becomes alive, fading in and out, as a soft whisper rises from the pages, saying: "Knowest the mystery, for if that which thy seekest thou findest not within thee, thou wilt never find it without thee."

Within your robe you feel the bag containing the three herbs given to you by the Kindred. Across the room you see the mortar and pestle sitting on a small table. You take the herbs over to the table and lay them out [Mortar and Pestle].

Intuitively you grind the herbs into a grainy powder, and then carefully fill the pouch within them.

Returning to the Book of Shadows, you sit with the pouch of herbs in hand. The pages of the book begin to turn as if by some unseen hand. They stop on a page titled Perfect Love and Perfect Trust [Perfect Love and Perfect Trust]. You realize that to possess knowledge one must trust the source, and that when knowledge becomes realization, then love is required before one can wield such power for the good of all with harm to none.

Holding the pouch of herbs in your left hand, you take hold of the elder staff with your right hand and begin to stand. You feel a power preventing this, and for a moment you feel two sets of hands pressing you back down to your seat. You sense that these are the hands of the priestess and priest. Your eyes become fixed on the Book of Shadows as though some explanation might appear.

The pages begin to turn slowly, and then stop on a page titled "Oath" [Oath]. On the page appears a face with one hand pressed upon it. One fingertip is placed below each eye. The words, "And as my word, so mote it be," appear bold and challenging. You realize that you must give your word, in trust and love, to serve others through what you have come to realize in your journey through the worlds.

You can still feel the hands upon your shoulders, but they are gentle now and you feel at peace. The voices of the priestess and priest whisper in your ears, "For what you know and what you share, some will love you and some will hate you. So has it been throughout time for all the messengers and keepers of knowledge and wisdom who came before you." You nod as though you understand, and truthfully, somewhere deep inside, you do comprehend.

You have not passed through test and trial to be loved or to be hated. Yours has been a seeker's truth for knowledge and wisdom. But you do not claim the gems for yourself, nor do you hide them away from others who are friend or foe. You have found the center, and at the center you reach out to connect with the world.

Exhausted, you lean forward, resting your head in your hand. You know that the journey ahead will follow a lonely path, for a vagabond of the Old Ways has no place to rest. You turn your eyes upward toward the Book of Shadows, and you chuckle softly, for your posture matches the illustration on the Oath page. There is nothing else to say but to utter the words, "And as my word, so mote it be."

Celebrating Seasonal Festivals

The eight seasonal ritual cards in this deck are ideal for solitary celebration. They can be used as a centerpiece, providing a focal point to celebrate or just simply acknowledge the seasonal rites of the Wheel of the Year. In addition, if you have a copy of *The Well Worn Path* divination cards, you can incorporate the festival cards from *The Hidden Path* into the solitary ritual layout. This appears on page 187 of the companion book for *The Well Worn Path*.

On the following pages you will find a simple setup for each festival, which can be used when time is an issue or privacy is a concern. This is also very practical for parents with small children, who have little time and energy left over at the end of the day. With just a little added creativity, some incense and candles, and a few decorations, you can enjoy the festival occasions throughout the year. It can be a great opportunity to teach your children about the Wheel of the Year, and it gives them a way to join in and learn about the connection of Nature to their lives while also establishing family traditions.

You will find this to be something you and your family look forward to.

It is best if you are able to go out into nature and gather the prescribed objects for the altar. Make an event of gathering up the items, even if it means going to a commercial "pumpkin patch" to purchase your autumn fruits or visiting your local park. If this is not possible, any well-stocked handcraft store should have everything you need.

In the art of each of the eight festival cards, you will notice the inclusion of a white, black, and red cord, which represents the Three Great Mysteries (birth, life, and death). The symbolism is a ritual tool that connects us to the seasonal turning of the Wheel of the Year. Physically creating a colored cord can make a vital connection to the flow of Nature. Everyone in the family can weave their own, or make one that is for the whole family. As a family project, each member braids a part of the cord.

Start with three cords, one of each color: white, red, and black. For the family cord it is best if each cord is nine feet in length. An individual's cord can be as short as three feet, but should be long enough to go around the waist. To begin, focus your attention on the seasonal symbolism and then tie all three cords together at one end. Begin braiding the cords downward. As you do this, say or chant the following:

> *Three mysteries do I here braid,*
> *connection to the Wheel is made.*
> *Birth, life, death, each has no end,*
> *an unbroken circle that begins again.*
>
> *I join the Wheel of Nature's way,*
> *with dark of night and light of day.*

The give and take of all held dear
within the waning and waxing year.

May this cord a joining be
to health, and love, and prosperity.
Endless blessings from the gods descend,
as the year's great Wheel turns yet again.

This charges the cords to be a connection for your intentions. When you reach the end of the cords, leave the same amount to tie off as you did on the other end. Now, you can anoint your cord with a magical oil, or pass it through incense smoke (or both). This now becomes the inner connection for the Wheel of the Year. To enhance the connections to the Wheel of the Year, you can tie one knot for each festival. Do this for each festival as it arrives, and continue until the year is complete. In this way you will have tied your experience to the cord eight times.

You can wear the cord, hold it in your hands, or place it on the altar as part of the ritual décor. With continued use the cord will become, over time, infused with the energies that you impart to it. You can create a family tradition of passing the cord on to future generations, and thereby ensure the survival of ancestral memories. Let's begin.

Samhain

Suggested Items

    The Samhain card (with a stand or prop
        to hold it up in place)
    Fall leaves

Several small gourds and pumpkins
Acorns
Pomegranates
A key
Red and black candles
A small dish for offerings
Photos of loved ones (including animals)
    who have crossed over
A small skull (to represent ancestors)
Halloween fun decorations

Select an area where you can set up the decorations. Use the Samhain card as a centerpiece. You can set it on something to make it stand higher than the surrounding decorations. Start by making a circle of fall-colored leaves around the card, and mix in small gourds, pomegranates, and pumpkins.

On the outer left and right of the decoration circle, place a red candle and a black candle. In the circle of leaves and fruits, off to the side of the Samhain card, place the photos or objects that represent your loved ones who have crossed over. In front of the card place an offering dish. Depending on your ancestral heritage, your may want to consider what to place as an offering. Typically, offerings represent a connection with the loved one. If Uncle Joe loved pretzels, put some pretzels in the dish. If your child's dog loved biscuit treats, then put the biscuits in the dish. Add the rest of the objects you would like to be a part of this seasonal altar using your own imagination and creativity.

Make time to sit and meditate on the card and the surrounding symbolism. Imagine that you are in the picture on the card. If you were actually there, what would you do or say? Think about prayers you want to offer, and things in your life that you wish to express appreciation for to the Goddess and God. Let the few moments you spend in front of the card and the decorations be a spiritual time for you. As with all things in life, the more you give the better the results.

Suggested Meditation

Sit before your altar, take three slow breaths in, and exhale out. Focus your attention on the Samhain card and the seasonal décor on your altar. Reflect on this as the first turn of the wheel. This is the beginning of the year in darkness and regeneration. It is the dark womb from which the New Year will be born. Samhain is the season of the opening of the veil between the worlds. The ancestral wisdom and knowledge of those who have gone before us is now possible to access.

Imagine the feel of the cool night air of Samhain Eve, and the smell of the heath fires and autumn leaves in the air. The full moon shines brightly in the night sky. The Goddess and God are present and she is adorned with the seasonal symbols. At her feet is a cauldron filled with the harvest of the season. The God's candle glows as it symbolizes his presence as her consort.

Kneeling before your altar, you see the skull of the ancestors lit with the candle of remembrance. The crossbones lie open to you as if outstretched arms are reaching to embrace you. You feel the breeze pick up and blow pass you. The time is here, and you speak these words:

I call to thee this sacred space,
by candle light I do embrace.
Give me moments to see,
and time to feel,
as I am part of Nature's Wheel.

Let your thoughts focus on Samhain as the time to make contact with those who have crossed the veil. Close your eyes and visualize the dark night. You begin to see a mist rolling toward you. You can see shapes in the mist. It is time to call to the ancestors for wisdom, knowledge, and the answers you seek. Allow yourself time to reach out to those you want to connect with; reflect on any messages you receive and ask for guidance for the coming year. You may want to write your thoughts down or keep an ongoing journal. Be sure to end with your offerings and thanks, and bid them farewell.

Yule/Winter Solstice

Suggested Items

The Yule card (with a stand or prop
    to hold it up in place)
Seasonal greenery: pine bough, mistletoe, holly,
    pinecones
Yule log (make 3 cut-outs for candles in the top)
Green candles
A small basket for the reed doll
Reed doll (make from raffia)
Symbol of the sun

Offering dish

Seasonal decorations such as ornaments

Select an area where you can set up the decorations. Use the Yule card as a centerpiece. Set it on something to make it stand higher than the surrounding decorations.

Start to decorate by creating a horseshoe shape with the seasonal greenery, starting from the front left and continuing around the back of the card and around to the right front. Place the Yule log in front of the card. Set three green candles in the holes in the Yule log. Next, place the basket with the doll in front of the Yule log. If you don't have an actual doll figure, place the sun symbol in the basket. In front of the card place your offering dish. Typically, offerings represent a connection at this time of year with renewal and new hope for the coming year. Add the rest of the objects you would like to be a part of this seasonal altar using your own imagination and creativity.

Suggested Meditation

Sit before your altar, take three slow breaths in and exhale out. Focus your attention on the Yule card (the winter solstice) and the seasonal décor on your altar. Reflect on this next turning of the wheel. This is the birth of the Child of Promise and the potential that awaits you. It is the divine spark within, bringing the promise of renewal, restoration, and rebirth. But for now all of Nature has receded to conserve its energy for the year ahead. Yule is the season when the Sun God returns, bringing the new light to revitalize the earth and all living things.

Imagine feeling relief at the return of the light of the new dawn. The chill of winter is in the air. The sun rises and shines upon the snowy ground. The God and Goddess are present and he is adorned with the seasonal symbols. The Goddess' candle glows as it symbolizes her presence as his consort. At her feet is her cauldron of rebirth, which is burning bright with the birthing fire of the new sun.

Kneeling before your altar, you see the reed basket containing the Child of Promise. You speak these words:

> *I call thee to this sacred space,*
> *by candle light I do embrace.*
> *Give me moments to see,*
> *and time to feel,*
> *as I am part of Nature's wheel.*

Reflect on Yule as the time to contemplate what the New Year may bring. Close your eyes and visualize the winter's rising sun on the horizon. You feel the new light penetrating the cold morning. It is time to draw within you and feel the divine spark that is flickering with new promise.

Allow yourself time to consider this season of conserving for the journey of the wheel ahead. Yule brings thoughts of what is worth preserving and what new actions you will take to bring renewal and restoration to the potential of your life in the coming year. Write your thoughts down.

Imbolc

Suggested Items

The Imbolc card (with a stand or prop
  to hold it up in place)

Raffia or reeds
White candles
White flowers
A small metal container for flammable liquid
A larger metal container or bowl (that can hold the
small bowl and allow extra space around it)
Offering dish
Seasonal decorations: Brid's Crosses and quartz crystals

Select an area where you can set up the decorations. Use the Imbolc card as a centerpiece. Set it on something to make it stand higher than the surrounding decorations. On the outer left and right of the decoration circle, place the white candles.

Create a reed bed in front of the Imbolc card. Place the larger container/bowl on top of the reed bed. Place the smaller container inside the larger one. On the eve of the festival night, put flammable liquid in the small container and ice cubes in the larger container (in effect, you will have fire in ice on your altar). Place your offering dish on the altar. Typically, offerings represent a connection at this time of year with purification and liberation. Add the rest of the objects you would like to be a part of this seasonal altar using your own imagination and creativity.

Suggested Meditation

Sit before your altar, take three slow breaths in, and exhale out. Focus your attention on the Imbolc card and the seasonal décor on your altar. Reflect on this continuing turn of the wheel. This is the time of purification and preparation. It is time to light the internal fire of transformation in order to release the potential frozen within. Imbolc is the season when the land is frozen, stagnant, and awaiting release.

Imagine feeling the frozen land. The air is so cold it is hard to breathe. The night is alight with a starry sky. The Goddess and God are present and she is adorned with the seasonal symbols. At her feet the cauldron of rebirth is glowing with the embers of the transformative fire. The God's candle glows as it symbolizes his presence as her consort.

Kneel before your altar and watch the fire flickering within the frozen block of ice. You sense that the fire longs to be freed from its limitation and you recognize that, once freed, the potential and expansion of power is great. You speak:

> *I call to thee this sacred space,*
> *by candle light I do embrace.*
> *Give me moments to see,*
> *and time to feel,*
> *as I am part of Nature's Wheel.*

Imbolc is the time to purify and make way for the work ahead. Close your eyes and visualize the fire burning away all obstacles and blocks. You feel the possibilities growing as you make room to expand and claim the new potential that awaits you. It is time to release, let go, and make way for the new desires you want to manifest. Allow yourself time to contemplate this season of purification and discernment for the journey of the wheel ahead. Imbolc brings you opportunity to make room for the coming year's harvest. Write your thoughts down.

Ostara/Spring Equinox

Suggested Items

The Ostara card (with a stand or prop
   to hold it up in place)
Green candles
Spring's first flowers
Colored eggs
Packets of seeds
Acorns
Offering dish
Seasonal decorations

Select an area where you can set up the decorations. Use the
Ostara card as a centerpiece (standing taller than the decorations). On the left and right of the altar, place the green candles. Place between the candles a vase of flowers that includes
reeds or cattails. Place the Ostara card in front of the vase.
Put your offering dish in the front of the card. The packets of
seeds you have chosen should symbolically represent what it
is you wish to manifest in this year's harvest. Place the seeds
in the offering dish. Typically, offerings represent a connection at this time of year with fertility, new plans, and gainful
projects. Now you can arrange the colored eggs and acorns
on the altar. Add the rest of the objects you would like to
be a part of this seasonal altar using your own imagination
and creativity.

Suggested Meditation

Sit before your altar; take three slow breaths in and exhale
out. Focus your attention on the Ostara card (the spring

equinox) and the seasonal décor on your altar. Reflect on this turn of the wheel. Tilling the soil, preparing the furrows, and planting seeds of growth for the new harvest is at hand. It is time to set goals for the year ahead so the harvest will be fruitful. Ostara is the season when the land is reawakening and signs of new life are beginning to appear.

Imagine feeling the resurgence of renewal returning to the land. The air is crisp and cool. The sun is rising in the sky and melting the snow upon the land. The God and Goddess are present and he is adorned with the seasonal symbols. The Goddess' candle glows as it symbolizes her presence as his consort. At the Goddess' feet, and from her cauldron of rebirth, rises magical mist that renews the earth, which has slept in the cold embrace of winter.

Kneel before your altar and see the symbols of new life waiting to be planted and spring forth with new growth. You feel the first stirrings of the growth that awaits you in the coming months. You speak:

> *I call to thee this sacred space,*
> *by candle light I do embrace.*
> *Give me moments to see,*
> *and time to feel,*
> *as I am part of Nature's Wheel.*

Ostara is the time to amend the soil and plant the seeds for new growth and the harvest ahead. Close your eyes and visualize the color of the rich soil, and the seeds of your harvest, blessed and ready for planting. You know the harvest will be abundant, as you have considered, observed, and prepared for this time to plant the seeds of your desired harvest. Allow yourself time to contemplate this season of planting and the work for the journey of the wheel ahead. Ostara brings you into the moment of taking action to begin the work that leads to the coming year's harvest. Write down your thoughts.

Beltane

Suggested Items

The Beltane card (with a stand or prop
   to hold it up in place)
Ivy
Flowers
Red candles
Wand
Shells
Phallic symbols
Offering dish
Seasonal decorations fertility symbols to enhance the
   seasonal growth

Select an area where you can set up the decorations. Use the Beltane card as a centerpiece, setting it on something to make it rise above the surrounding decorations. On the outer left and right of the decoration circle, place the red candles.

Create a circle of ivy in front of the Beltane card. In the circle place an arrangement of flowers of the season, including red and white roses. In front of the circle of ivy, place a wand. Place your offering dish on the altar. Typically, offerings represent a connection at this time of year with new relationships, positive attitudes, and self-improvements. Add the rest of the objects you would like to be a part of this seasonal altar using your own imagination and creativity.

Suggested Meditation

Sit before your altar, take three slow breaths in, and exhale out. Focus your attention on the Beltane card and the seasonal décor on your altar. Reflect on this turn of the wheel. The forces of Nature bring out the passion and desire of the soul. It is time to be passionate, and move forward with desires and action for manifestation. Beltane is the season when the land is fertile and brings new life.

Imagine the sense of mystery and feel the excitement of life returning to the land. The air is filled with the fragrance of flower blossoms and fireflies light the night. The sky is bright with stars. The Goddess and God are present and she is adorned with the seasonal symbols. At her feet is a cauldron filled with flower blossoms. In front of the cauldron appears the fallen antler of the God, symbolizing the passing of his reign into the Goddess' hands. The God's candle glows as it symbolizes his presence as her consort.

Kneeling before your altar, you see the symbols of fertility and union before you. You feel the forces of Nature bringing passion and desire to life.

You speak:

> *I call to thee this sacred space,*
> *by candle light I do embrace.*
> *Give me moments to see,*
> *and time to feel,*
> *as I am part of Nature's Wheel.*

Beltane is the time when magic is in the air and you are filled with excitement. Close your eyes and visualize the land green with the vitality of new life. You feel electricity in the air, with the newness of growth and potential beginning to manifest. It is a time to be passionately focused on your goals and continue to tend, with fervor, the manifestation of your harvest. Allow yourself the time to contemplate this season of potential and desire in the journey of the wheel ahead. Beltane brings you into the moment of owning the passion and desires of life. Write your thoughts down.

Litha/Summer Solstice

Suggested Items

> The Litha card (with a stand or prop
>   to hold it up in place)
> A small cake, decorated in red and white
> Green candles
> Red and white roses or other flowers
> Flower petals
> Mistletoe (if available)
> Wheat sheaves
> 2 chalices or cups
> Offering dish
> Seasonal decorations: wedding symbols

Select an area where you can set up the decorations. Use the Litha card as a centerpiece. Set it on something to make it stand higher than the surrounding decorations. On the outer left and right sides of the Litha card, place the green candles. In front of the Litha card, place the wedding cake.

On either side of the wedding cake, place flowers. Place the two chalices in front of and on both sides of the wedding cake. Wine is best, but feel free to use whatever celebratory drink is appropriate for you and family members. Spread the wheat sheaves, rose petals, and mistletoe around the cake.

Place your offering dish on the altar. Typically, offerings represent a connection at this time of year with social activities, tending and cultivating, and appreciating the blessings in your life. Select the rest of the objects you would like to be a part of this seasonal altar using your own imagination and creativity.

Suggested Meditation

Sit before your altar; take three slow breaths in, and exhale out. Focus your attention on the Litha card (the summer solstice) and the seasonal décor on your altar. Reflect on this turn of the wheel. The divine couple is joined together in marriage. Nature is acknowledging the success of the work that has been done so far. It is time to celebrate the union of the divine couple and the effort that has ensured this bountiful time in your life. Litha is the season when the land is abundant and potency can be seen all around you.

Imagine feeling the hot sun on your skin. The air is dry and there is a sweetness aloft. The sun is shining high in the sky. The God and Goddess are present and he is adorned with the seasonal symbols. The Goddess' candle glows, symbolizing her presence as his consort. At her feet is a cauldron filled with ripe wheat sheaves. The divine couple is joined as one with the cord of the mysteries signifying their union.

Kneeling before your altar, you see the symbols of celebration and union before you. You feel the welling up of harmony, fulfillment, accomplishment, and the potency of the season. You speak:

> *I call to thee this sacred space,*
> *by candle light I do embrace.*
> *Give me moments to see,*
> *and time to feel,*
> *as I am part of Nature's Wheel.*

Litha is the time when the divine couple is united and celebration of the land begins. Close your eyes and visualize the God and Goddess joined in union as the sun and the land are connected together for the coming harvest. You feel the accomplishment of the first steps toward realizing your harvest, which grows ever closer. You recognize that the work done equals the results obtained. It is a time to celebrate and acknowledge the vitality within the process of Nature. Allow yourself time to contemplate this season of harmony and fulfillment, and the joy of the continuing journey of the wheel ahead. Litha brings you into the moment of celebration and anticipation of the process of life. Write down your thoughts.

Lughnasadh

Suggested Items

The Lughnasadh card (with a stand or prop
   to hold it up in place)
Cornucopia

Seasonal fruits
Pale yellow candles
Offering dish
Rosemary, lavender, and rue
Seasonal decorations: symbols of your harvest

Select an area where you can set up the decorations. Use the Lughnasadh card as a centerpiece. Set it on something to make it stand higher than the surrounding decorations. On the outer left and right side of the Lughnasadh card, place the yellow candles.

Place the cornucopia on the altar table, and arrange the bounty in the cornucopia and spill it out onto the altar. Place the herbs, tied together in bundles, on the altar.

Place your offering dish on the altar. Typically, offerings represent a connection at this time of year with preparation and receptivity. Add the rest of the objects you would like to be a part of this seasonal altar using your own imagination and creativity.

Suggested Meditation

Sit before your altar, take three slow breaths in and exhale out. Focus your attention on the Lughnasadh card and the seasonal décor on your altar. Reflect on this turn of the wheel. The bounty of Nature is nearing its journey's end, but there still remains the final work to do. It is time to prepare for a successful harvest. Lughnasadh is the season when the land is ripening but has yet to reach the fullness to come.

Imagine feeling the calm and fragrant night. The air is filled with the aroma of the fields, which fills your senses.

The moon is half lit in the starry sky. The Goddess and God are present and she is adorned with the seasonal symbols. At her feet is a cauldron filled with fruit, which represent the full ripeness of the womb of the Goddess. The God's candle glows as it symbolizes his presence as her consort.

Kneeling before your altar, you see the fruits of your labor. You understand that the work you have been doing throughout the year has brought the abundance that is now set before you. But you also know there is still one last surge of effort. You speak:

> *I call to thee this sacred space,*
> *by candle light I do embrace.*
> *Give me moments to see,*
> *and time to feel,*
> *as I am part of Nature's Wheel.*

Lugnasadh is the time when the first harvest awaits and is savored in its own right. Close your eyes and visualize the manifestation of the bounty of your efforts and work. You feel an amazing satisfaction in understanding that the process of growth takes time and attention in order to achieve the desired results. Now is the time for enjoyment of the fruits of the harvest and the preparation for the final threshing. Allow yourself time to contemplate this season of fulfillment and the growth you have experienced thus far. The anticipation of the harvest is at hand. Lughnasadh brings you into the moment of enjoying the fruits of your labor and a final expectation of the journey's end. Write your thoughts down.

Mabon/Autumn Equinox

Suggested Items

    The Mabon card (with a stand or prop
       to hold it up in place)
    Reed or raffia basket used at Yule
    White candles
    Grain stalks
    Small pumpkins
    Apples
    Acorns
    Cakes of grain
    Offering dish
    Seasonal decorations: symbols of your final harvest

Select an area where you can set up the decorations. Use the Mabon card as a centerpiece, setting it on something to make it stand higher than the surrounding decorations. Core out two apples, the diameter of the altar candles. Place the white candles in the apples, and put them on the outer left and right sides of the Mabon card. Place the basket on the altar and fill it with the grain cakes and wheat stalks. Spread the apples and pumpkins around the basket.

Place your offering dish on the altar. Typically offerings represent a connection at this time of year with harvest and fulfillment. Add the rest of the objects you would like to be a part of this seasonal altar, using your own imagination and creativity.

Suggested Meditation

Sit before your altar. Take three breaths in and exhale out. Focus your attention on the Mabon card (the autumn equinox) and the seasonal décor on your altar. This journey's end has culminated in the harvest. With this come the seeds for the next season's turn of the wheel. Birth, life, death, and renewal begin anew. It is time to rejoice in the completion of the season with celebration, reflection, and enjoyment of the abundance of the harvest. Mabon is the season when the land has reached its full ripeness and is ready to be gathered in.

Feel the Indian Summer on a fall afternoon. The air feels warm and dry like the leaves on the trees. The sun is setting and its light casts shadows. The God and Goddess are present and he is adorned with the seasonal symbols. The Goddess' candle glows as it symbolizes her presence as his consort. At her feet is an empty cauldron with nine white shells set in front. The sickle represents completion of the harvest. The raven atop the sickle is the messenger that flies between the worlds.

Kneel before your altar; the manifestation of your "seeds" is before you. You have reached and achieved your goals and harvest for this season. You have experienced the mystery of birth-life-death in one complete turn of the wheel. You speak:

> *I call to thee this sacred space,*
> *by candle light I do embrace.*
> *Give me moments to see,*

and time to feel,
as I am part of Nature's Wheel.

Mabon is the time when the work has been accomplished and the harvest is complete. Close your eyes and experience the pleasure of seeing the manifestation, accomplishment, and fulfillment of your desire. You feel a connection to Nature that brings an appreciation of knowing you and Nature are one and the same. The turning of the wheel through the seasons has aligned you with the cycles of birth, life, and death. You have gained the insight to know now that rebirth and renewal are ensured, for you and Nature are one. It is a time to take pleasure, and acknowledge what you have gained from your journey. Allow yourself time to contemplate this season of completion and achievement. Mabon brings you to the end of this journey, and leaves you with the seeds and time to envision the next journey of the wheel. Write your thoughts down.

To Write to the Authors

If you wish to contact the authors or artist, or would like more information about this book, please write to the author in care of Llewellyn Worldwide and we will forward your request. The authors, artist, and publisher appreciate hearing from you and learning of your enjoyment of this book and how it has helped you. Llewellyn Worldwide cannot guarantee that every letter written to the authors or artist can be answered, but all will be forwarded. Please write to:

Raven Grimassi and Stephanie Taylor
Llewellyn Worldwide
2143 Wooddale Drive, Dept. 978-0-7387-1070-9
Woodbury, Minnesota 55125-2989, U.S.A.

Please enclose a self-addressed stamped envelope for reply,
or $1.00 to cover costs. If outside U.S.A., enclose
international postal reply coupon.

Many of Llewellyn's authors have websites with additional information and resources. For more information, please visit our website at http://www.llewellyn.com.